Christmas 1981

D0008059

Nancy,

I am really enjoying this book. It's a real encouragement to me, & I hope you'll enjoy it, too. (The author is a Wheaton grad.)

Ps. 37.5

With love,
Mary Ellen

Keep These Things,
Ponder Them in Your Heart

MIRIAM HUFFMAN ROCKNESS

Keep These Things,
Ponder Them in Your Heart

REFLECTIONS OF A MOTHER

A DOUBLEDAY-GALILEE ORIGINAL

DOUBLEDAY & COMPANY, INC., GARDEN CITY, NEW YORK   1979

Permission to quote material from the following sources is gratefully acknowledged:

Milambu Ya Bababa used by permission of John Knox Press. "I Meant to Do My Work Today" reprinted by permission of Dodd, Mead & Company, Inc. from *The Lonely Dancer* by Richard Le Gallienne. Copyright 1913 by Dodd, Mead & Company, Inc. Copyright renewed 1941 by Richard Le Gallienne.

"You're Something Special." Words by William J. and Gloria Gaither and music by William J. Gaither. © Copyright 1974 by William J. Gaither. International copyright secured. All rights reserved. Used by permission.

"Through It All" by Andrae Crouch. © Copyright 1971 by Manna Music, Inc., 2111 Kenmere Ave., Burbank, CA 91504. International copyright secured. All Rights Reserved. Used by Permission.

"Fog" reprinted from *Complete Poems* by Carl Sandburg, copyright 1916 by Holt, Rinehart and Winston, Inc.; copyright 1944 by Carl Sandburg. Reprinted by Permission of Harcourt Brace Jovanovich, Inc.

Selections from *The New Testament in Modern English*, Rev. Edn., by J. B. Phillips reprinted with permission of Macmillan Publishing Co., Inc. © J. B. Phillips 1958, 1960, 1972.

To Dave,
for this is really our book

Contents

Introduction

It is easier to say what this book is not than to say what it is. It is not a "how to." I'm qualified by neither training nor experience. It is not a comprehensive statement on motherhood. Still in the formative stages myself, with children one and a half, four, and seven years of age, I lack the perspective of one who can see the whole.

What then would possess one with my apparent lack of qualifications to write a book? The same as the above. That's all. I am a mother. And in my very lack of expertise I share common ground with those for whom I write, mothers who like me are "in process." We bear so awesome a responsibility, not by merit or qualification but by the design of our Creator. It is a vocation of reverse order—we take on the job and then learn to do it. Much like throwing a non-swimmer into water. A sink-or-swim proposition. Did God know what He was doing when He put so precious a charge into our young, inexperienced care?

This is a book of reflections. Reflections on the frustrations, struggles, questions, fears, joys unique to this stage of mothering. I feel there is value in sharing my efforts to cope, while I'm here. It is so easy to forget. Every mother will identify with the satisfactions of this stage. We tend to remember the happy moments above all. Rightfully so!

I did not become an adult when I left home at twenty-one years of age. But I assumed adult responsibilities. In the following ten years I made a lifelong commitment in marriage to the man I love, launched a career as a teacher, made three major moves, and brought three children into this world. Transitional years, these years. I read, questioned, observed, stumbled, and picked myself up again and again in my efforts to put it all together.

In part it was sport, this business of finding myself as a person. Being on my own. Testing my limits while still young and optimistic.

But it was in having children of my own that life took on new dimensions. Serious business, this matter of preparing children to survive in an adult world.

What are my responsibilities to my children? To my husband? To society? To myself? Where do I look for answers? Not theories. They are not enough now. Truth . . . And what about my failings? Are they redeemable? That's where I am. That's what this book is about.

Here then are my thoughts—activated from everyday experiences; colored by the bias of my life situation; written from a porch swing, a kitchen table, a back porch step, sitting on the floor next to a baby perched on a potty (waiting, waiting, waiting), on refined early mornings before the rest of the family awakened, or during that priceless naptime.

Is it absurd to think these intensely personal, highly individual reflections could be of interest to others? Friends, perhaps—but strangers? Could my experience possibly be of value to anyone else?

As I listen to other women, I have become increasingly aware of the common threads that run through the fabric of our individual lives. While the specific details that shape our existence may separate us, the differences are transcended by similar concerns and similar solutions.

So I share my process. If it triggers for someone else insights into their own life situations, it will more than justify the writing of these reflections.

Open Letter to My Mother

Dear Mother,

I'm sitting in the back yard watching Kimberly so intent on her little-girl play. She is making acorn soup in her yellow bucket. To her mud water stock she adds a blade of grass, five acorns, two brown leaves, then seasons it with sand. After stirring her brew with a stick, she leaves it to cook hanging in a sunny spot from a branch of a tree. My childhood seems so close to me when I see my daughter at play. What will she remember of the big and little events that make up her childhood? Will she forget as much as I have forgotten? I want to give back to you some of my memories—memories which today shape my desire to create for my children a home in the deepest sense of the word. So I'm writing you this open letter—not only as a tribute but also as an example to others in a time when we are so wanting for models.

Looking back I realize you had a basic commitment to our childhood—you understood the nature of the child and created an environment fitting for his nurture. Our life was made up of routines. Daily—mealtimes, naps, bedtimes. Weekly—piano lessons, Saturday's traditional Boston baked bean dinner, and Sunday's church activities and leisure. Yearly—our annual pilgrimage to Indiana and our eager return home after a full lakeside summer. These routines were a part of our given—at points challenged, yet essentially accepted. We came to know what we could expect. There was a certainty about life from which we derived an enormous sense of security.

Variety was the embroidery on the routine fabric of our life. Superimposed onto our routine pattern was the out-of-the-ordinary—

the Very Special. Breaking up late-afternoon play for church may have been met with resistance but not resentment, for there was the very real possibility of ice cream at Brigham's after church or a special treat upon returning home. Bedtime was thrown to the winds when Father's return from a trip was celebrated with popcorn, shiny apples, and water brimming with ice cubes savored around a crackling fire. The emphasis on daily meals may have been nutrition (little appreciated by us), but then there was always Sunday noon dinner. No company was ever treated better than us! The appetizer was served on a silver tray in the living room—fruit juice with a blob of sherbet and wafers. In the dining room we ate our "company meal" from our finest china and silver and finished it off with a spectacular dessert tantalizingly displayed on a pedestal server. And you served tea from the lusterware tea set in a performance equaled only by a traditional Japanese tea ceremony! I suspect now that you were creating an atmosphere for the leisurely sharing of ideas and good conversation.

How we anticipated the holidays and special days—each and every one. You took these occasions and turned them into events which instantly were declared Traditions: back-to-school shopping, pumpkin-carving, Thanksgiving dinner, all those special details that made up Christmas, Lincoln log cake for Dad's February 12 birthday, setting out spring plants and window boxes, shopping for summer clothes (and the style show upon return home), Fourth of July watermelon search (with Dad insisting on a center cut from each potential melon—much to our embarrassment) . . .

Add to that the element of serendipity: unexpected company, excursions, trips, notes tucked in my mirror on a significant day, a gift for no reason at all. Then there was my birthday, that one special day set aside to celebrate my being alive! The pink heart cake for my "almost Valentine" birthday, the florist arriving with a nosegay of fresh violets, a dainty heart-shaped box or violet-related gift. To this day violets, hearts, and the color pink in some way remind me that I'm someone special.

That our home was indeed safe and free from major tragedy I know now was a blessing and not a guarantee. But I feel you gave me the ability to cope with—even value—the ordinariness of life and the skill to create adventure out of the everyday resources around me.

You felt a child's play was his "work" and toys were the "equipment" and you chose carefully the few toys we owned. We, too, took them seriously and they opened all kinds of avenues for creative expression. I still have most of my toys—the Little Women dolls, the Singer sewing machine, the Ginny dolls with their lovely wardrobes, the miniature tea set, the little rocking chair now sitting in Kimberly's room, and the doll house presented to me on my fifth Christmas which you gradually furnished with exquisite wooden miniatures. (Remember how I traded all my wooden furniture for my neighbor's shiny plastic set and how heartbroken I was that you made me an Indian giver by reclaiming them?) I had the freedom to stake off my territory in our unfinished basement. There I could mother a kitten, set up a clubhouse, publish neighborhood newspapers, produce plays, and organize book fairs . . . I don't recall your involvement in these activities as much as your making available the raw materials.

You provided opportunities for us that were the testing grounds for interests some of which are an important part of my life today. I think back on my subscription to *Jack & Jill* magazine. Oh, how I anticipated its monthly arrival in the mail! I'd devour its contents immediately and before the week was over I'd begin my daily check of the mail for my next edition. Then there was the year I was a member of a record club . . . Rainy days and late Saturday afternoons set the stage to pull out the record player from the radio cabinet and play my "very own" records. I learned every story line and sang each song by heart from sheer repetition. With an occasional cue I think I could perform them now!

I can't honestly say I had any idea how unique an experience my grade-school piano lessons were, but once I came to weekly terms with my loss of a Saturday morning, I boarded the bus with an almost euphoric sense of independence and forgot myself in the lessons, water-coloring room, mini-concerts, and lunch in the walled gardens of the stately Longy School of Music in Cambridge. Could that have been the beginning of my present enjoyment of the arts?

16

I did know I was one lucky girl to have a harp and loved our Saturday "lesson morning" in Chicago throughout my high school years. What a joy it was to select records to play in the listening rooms at Lyon and Healy and to browse through the books at Kroch's and Brentano's. We did know how to make the most of those lessons!

I know you almost had to force me on every trip we took—whether to California or the Middle East—so content I was to stay put. But once on my way I enjoyed myself as much for the concentrated family time as for the expanding experiences. (I can almost hear you saying, "I told you someday you'd appreciate our insistence.") These opportunities had their cost and, I know, involved definite sacrifices from you, but how they enriched my life.

Just as meaningful were the experiences you provided for us that had comparatively no cost—those excursions you called "memory building": picnics at Wellesley, the historical blitz of New England before our move to the Midwest (Louisa May Alcott's home, Longfellow's Wayside Inn, Emerson's and Thoreau's homes, swan boat rides at the Boston Garden), the walks along a brook from Arlington to Belmont, watching the sun set across the lake, touring the streets of Beacon Hill to see the Christmas lights. Your exasperating insistence that we pay attention to detail has paid off, for I find myself bringing to our children's awareness the green, green of new leaves, bird song, a single rosebud, a clay pot filled with tulips forced into early bloom, the scent of perfume, the feel of clean sheets, the beauty of hand-painted china, the soft glow of old silver—all those things that can lift our spirits and that are ours to enjoy if not to possess. There may be many opportunities we may not be able to provide, things we cannot own, but you have shown me in no uncertain terms that richness of the spirit does not depend on financial resources.

While you gave careful attention to a positive home atmosphere, your real emphasis was on the development of character. There was never a question in my mind that the "inner I" mattered far more than anything I could achieve or accomplish. "What I am to be, I am now becoming," you quoted till it made its groove in my young, impressionable mind. I know you surrounded me with every positive influence you could possibly conceive of.

"Books are our friends," you said, and you proved it by reading to yourself and to us and by seeing that we were surrounded with books. I considered it the grandest treat to walk "all by myself" to the library. Fondly I recall how, as a family, we read the *Junior Pilgrim's Progress* and shared insights into the walk of life through Pilgrim's misadventures and discoveries. You often marked special occasions with the presentation of a carefully chosen book, thoughtfully inscribed. Books *are* my friends; I never fail to feel a warm glow as I am reminded of the contents of a dearly loved book by a glance at its cover, and in every room of the house I have surrounded myself with these good friends.

Yet you saw *life* as the real arena for character development, and you dealt with each situation as it presented itself. I've observed in facing the difficult situations in our children's lives that there are two general approaches. One is to resent these conflicts as intruders; the other is to consider them as opportunities to deal with and work through life situations. You took our problems, conflicts, and wrongdoings as the stuff out of which characters are shaped. Not long ago I was browsing through my childhood library when the well-worn book in my hand fell open to a chapter on honesty. My mind went back to your efforts to help a five-year-old, big into lying, distinguish between make-believe and real. To this day, any lie—black, gray, or white—jolts my conscience, made sensitive by your indoctrination.

My fearful nature must have been an endless source of frustration to you. But there was no outward indication of that the time our mother-daughter outing was so abruptly ended by my certainty that I saw a louse crawl down my leg. On the desperate ride home you unearthed from me that it wasn't just that one louse I feared, but the diagnosis made by a close friend earlier that day that my cat had lice, and the accompanying prediction that I would certainly catch them, that they would multiply in my hair, which would, in turn, have to be shaved off. You'll never know my relief when later you looked down at me in the bathtub and finally declared with every outward sign of seriousness "all clear" after examining every square inch of my quivering little body.

18

It must have demanded a special measure of wisdom to discern when sympathy or firmness was in order. My shyness in junior high required that kind of wisdom. Having moved from Massachusetts to Illinois I was filled with loneliness, uncertainty, and self-doubt. Every day after school I poured out my woes and you comforted and reassured me. I was certain that everyone else had his own friends and I had nothing to offer. I will never forget the day, much later on, when you took a different tactic. "Miriam," you said, "I have listened and understood. But the time has come when I must make something clear to you. At the very heart of shyness is selfishness. You have made your concern for yourself so important that you are failing to think about others." You continued on and concluded with this challenge. "There is someone in your school who is worse off than you. Tomorrow when you feel so uncertain, you look until you find that person and you be to them what you are looking for others to be to you." I could see she meant business and that sympathy had come to an end. That took courage, and involved risk. To this day when a situation looks too big for me, I look for that one person more uncertain than myself.

Then there was the time I made that $50 pledge in response to a particularly heart-rending plea for money when I had no apparent source of income. By indenturing me for one year of floor-scrubbing and fixture-cleaning you provided for me a means to fulfill this commitment. While I can't say this experience instilled in me the joy of giving, it did teach me the seriousness of a promise. You dealt with situations as they came up, regardless of how time-consuming or inconvenient.

You taught us to take seriously our relationship as a family. We were required to treat each family member with at least the same interest and respect as we would our friends. After all, "How can we expect to get along with others if we don't first learn to live with those closest to us?" Communication was fundamental in our family. You made an art of listening, and through listening you conveyed to us a sense of our worth. As we expressed our thoughts, ideas took form, issues were clarified, problems were sorted out. Family members were given equal time so we experienced the discipline of listening while gaining insight and support from the group mind. You encouraged us to "go deeper," to keep in touch with ourselves through writing a journal of thoughts yet too vulnerable to risk with each other.

You introduced us to another dimension of communication as you sought to put us in touch with our Creator through your example and guidance. Daily you prayed for the specific details of our lives and encouraged us to do the same. Early one morning, lured by the sound of my name, I stood eavesdropping on the other side of the bedroom door as you and Father prayed aloud. My curiosity won out and I asked you what you prayed for me. You said that among other things you were praying for the boy who would someday be my husband. To a twelve-year-old girl, whose relationship with boys was limited to awkward smiles and daydreams, this was an overwhelming thought. Later that day I knelt at my bedside and prayed. Determined to put in my "two bits," I detailed to God my ideal man. Suddenly sobered by the gap between my "ideal man" and the "real me" I prayed that I would grow to be worthy of the kind of man I would want to marry. A person to whom faith has never come easily, I have had my questions and struggles. Yet even in my times of darkest doubts the integration of your faith into everyday living has offered a convincing evidence of its reality.

You helped me identify positively with being a woman in a world where there is such uncertainty. You encouraged me from childhood to prepare for a career outside the home and to utilize this training. But you recognized the very real possibility that there might be years consumed with home-based responsibilities. You invested the role of homemaker with dignity, and provided me with experiences that were as much a training for homemaking as were my four college years for teaching. Value, you taught, came not from the job, but how that job was done. Somehow knowing that I do have options has made making difficult choices easier. Sometimes the choices involve giving up something I want for something I value even more. And I'm discovering life is made up of choices that are not only between good and bad but between good and good, and that these quality-of-life choices have more to do with being a person than being a woman.

This letter would not be complete without mentioning those

last college years at home. Up until that time it seemed that there was no situation too difficult—no problem that did not have a solution. Now I was to watch you deal with serious financial reverses over which you had no control. I watched you learn to live with a crisis that seemed to have no end—the only change was further complications. Life took on new dimensions for me as I came to grips with the fact that things don't always turn out as planned, that "if only's" don't count, and that sometimes there are no easy answers. As I saw you deal with the given of your situation, I began to learn the greatest lessons yet about life. You claimed that God does not give tasks equal to our power, but power equal to our tasks, and went on to live one day at a time, joyfully, while still working through the larger situation. And I observed that life could be lived above the circumstances rather than dominated by the circumstances. As a family we began to distinguish between big and little problems and, in doing so, became increasingly grateful for how much we had of what really mattered. We began to distinguish between dealing with a problem and dwelling on the problem, thus putting the needless, emotion-draining aspects to rest with an act of the will. You helped us come to value testing and trials as necessary experiences in the "growth of a soul."

You invested in our lives with the intention of preparing us to become adults—to be ultimately independent of you. As children, we were held in a tight fist which gradually opened until, with your hand extended, we were to walk off, however tentatively, as adults. Your investment in my life, as you helped me deal with life's given, both good and bad, has more than prepared me to accept the responsibility for my own life. I guess that is what being an adult is all about.

I realize that part of this transition from childhood to adulthood involved analyzing and criticizing the way you did things. This seemed to be a necessity in the process of distinguishing who I was from who you were. But it is having children of my own that has made me aware of just what was involved in your parenting.

On my graduation day you left a letter in my room reviewing my life up to that point. Much of what you said then is taking on greater meaning to me at age thirty-three, as I can now begin to look back at the ups and downs of my life. You concluded your letter—so rich in reminiscence—by saying:

. . . Miriam, Father and I count it a privilege to call you our daughter. I would wish for you in the years ahead the experience of having a daughter of your own.

Our children are the living monuments we shall leave behind in life and naturally our uppermost desire is for you to bring honor to God. As you dwell in His Word daily and, through prayer, faithfully yield yourself in obedience to His will, this will be so.

When you receive your diploma today, and next Friday, your special day you've been waiting for through the years when you receive your wedding ring from Dave, you will in a real sense be graduated from your school days and childhood home, but never from our thoughts and prayers. As God gives us breath we shall continue to bring you before Him every single day in prayer.

Remember, the future holds nothing, nothing for which God's love has not made provision.

I can leave you nothing better than Joshua 1:8, 9 for the days ahead.

Affectionately,
Mother

Thank you for the kind of mother you have been to me.

Lovingly,
Miriam

1

*Home—"A Safe Place"**

"Looking back I realize you had a basic commitment to our childhood—you understood the nature of the child and created an environment fitting for his nurture. There was a certainty about life from which we derived an enormous sense of security."

* Gladys Hunt, MS *Means Myself*.

BUILDING OUR NEST

Home. Something deep within me responds in warm recognition as I round the corner and park the car in the shade of a giant oak tree. A passer-by would see a gray clapboard house trimmed in white. They'd notice the red door. The picket fence. Maybe the window box spilling over with red impatiens. A charming house—to those who appreciate the 1920 vintage of the South—with its roomy porch sprawling clear across the front.

I walk up the steps softly chanting Mr. Bird's song from our children's beloved book *The Best Nest*:

> *I love my house*
> *I love my nest*
> *In all the world*
> *My nest is best.*[1]

It's become "our song." I sing it with conviction. I love this house. It is *home*.

It was not always so. But I'll start from the beginning. Five years ago we picked up all our earthly possessions, including one baby (and one in the making) and relocated a thousand miles south in a place where we were strangers. Too soon to have grown roots, far from all that was familiar, I was in emotional suspension. Even my childhood home no longer existed in the same sense due to the recent move of my parents. Every home I had ever lived in was occupied by strangers. There was no place I could relate to, even emotionally, as home. For the first time in my life I was totally without "a place of my own."

Time passed. Fall came—90 degrees in the shade. People insisted that the heat wave during the Christmas holidays was unseasonable. Where were the spring flowers? And then there was summer . . . Yes, summer! People would ask, "Have you got sand in your shoes yet?" I would numbly smile and murmur noncommittally. They had touched on something much deeper than they could ever know. They asked with such assurance, the assurance of those who alone had a place. How could they know what I was experiencing—"placelessness."

I read about homes. As we'd drive I'd feast my eyes on houses that looked like homes. Mentally I rebuked my parents for "desertion." I fantasized about a perfect place for us. And observed with envy families living out their lives surrounded by several generations. They have what I'll never have.

I was wrong. But it took a devastating moment of truth to wake me up. It took The Christmas That Almost Wasn't. My parents' holiday visit was dependent on "how Grandmother is doing." And she wasn't "doing" well. When we hadn't heard otherwise by the day before Christmas, I concluded we'd be alone. I accepted friends' invitation for Christmas dinner and simultaneously made another decision. Why even bother with the house? It's "just us." Why clean? Why bake? Who cares if the dry evergreens are replaced? I distributed my remaining Christmas cookies throughout the neighborhood in an attempt to simulate the Christmas spirit. As I walked in from my mission the phone was ringing.

"All's set." It was Father's hearty voice. "We'll be arriving in exactly four hours! Merry Christmas!"

Merry Christmas! How could I pull together anything that would faintly resemble Christmas in four hours? I looked around at a house that looked like the Week After and was duly humbled. A flashback from my childhood came into sharp focus . . .

It was Christmas Eve day. The entire family was united in one goal—to pull everything together in time to take our annual tour of lights. I was delegated to the cleaning of my room. (Now, with present mother insight, I suspect I had been removed from the scene.) I took on my cleaning with zeal. Not only did I clean the visible, but emptied my closet and painstakingly rearranged its contents. Next I tackled my dresser drawers. With the same dedication I launched into the cleaning of my doll house. Not one surface, not one piece of furniture went untouched. The final task was cleaning me. I soaked myself clean in a tub brimming with warm sudsy water.

Order finally emerged from chaos and we went off with high spirits. But it was when we returned to our house that I first felt the magic. A soft blanket of snow erased all imperfections. In each window shone a single candle. The wreath bedecked with berries and a red satin bow hung on the door. Through the window I could see the tinseled tree strung with cranberries and popcorn. I scarcely dared to breathe for fear of breaking the spell.

In a haze of wonder I was transported from car to bed. After loving good-nights I lay in my bed, propped on two pillows, blankets up to my chin. I remember first the overwhelming sense of cleanness. Clean room, clean sheets, clean pajamas, clean me.

I settled back and basked in the perfection of this moment. Sounds of my parents' activity downstairs—rustling paper, muted conversation. I pictured the fire dancing and leaping in the fireplace. A cut-glass bowl filled with pink popcorn balls. The tiny snow-frosted village under the Christmas tree.

Then I drank in the loveliness of my room. It was softly bathed in light from candles in the windows. Light shone from the windows of my doll house. A wreath hung on its door. Outside, snowflakes made their gentle descent. I snuggled deeper into my freshly ironed sheets. So warm inside. The warmth was more than physical. I was intoxicated with happiness. This was certainly the most wonderful moment of my life. I savored every detail in an effort to etch it forever in my mind. Life could never exceed this. Solemnly I vowed to extend this moment by staying awake all night. That was the last thing I remember . . .

One perfect moment. One moment born of someone's love and giving. Perhaps sacrifice. One moment remembered out of the many forgotten moments lost to consciousness, but were they not the materials from which strong emotional building blocks were formed?

I thought about my children. My husband. What was I doing to create a home in the deepest sense of the word for them? Were they not worthy of the same efforts that had been made for me? I will always attribute to our crossing of wires this moment of truth: I was still looking to others to receive something which had been given to me. But the time had come for me to give. I realized fully, for the first time, that all those good things that went into forming a home didn't just happen. *Someone* had to invest love, energy, and creative thought. Rather than looking elsewhere for the perfect place, the time had come that my place, wherever it was, would simply have to become home. And someone would have to shape that home out of the stuff of the here and now. That someone was *me*.

Amazingly, there was a semblance of order when my parents promptly arrived four hours later. But that feat was not the most significant thing that had taken place. As I cleaned and polished and added special touches throughout the house, an important change in perspective had taken place in my heart. Instead of vainly longing for a place for me, I would create a place for those I loved.

There was no instant transformation. Rather, the beginning of a "process" based on a commitment to the bigger picture. And in that picture I was the artist creating a "safe place." Exactly what that would involve was yet to be discovered. But what had seemed too great an effort only hours before was now elevated by a broader understanding of how it fit into the whole. The Christmas That Almost Wasn't became the first twig in the grander scheme—the building of "our nest."

IN DEFENSE OF THE ORDINARY

Back to school! Today is the big day. David and Kimberly were the first to greet the morning. They entered into the preparations with enthusiastic abandon. David, assuming a jaunty air of self-assurance, took the full responsibility of readying himself for school. Big second-grader, he! I dressed Kimberly in her blue, eyelet-trimmed dress; tied red ribbons around her ponytails. "I'm going to learn the letter people this year, aren't I?" She has finally reached the top rung of the nursery school ladder. Breakfast for the children. Teeth-brushing ceremony. Goodbye kisses. At last they were off—David clutching his new lunchbox, pencil box tucked under his arm; Kimberly bouncing along, her feet scarcely touching the ground. Even Jonathan was a part of the action, off to his morning with the "run-abouts"—lesson number one in social development!

Dave and I celebrated with breakfast out. Back at home I gave the house a once-over. Swept the porches and walks. Dumped a load of clothing in the washing machine.

Now I sit on the screened porch and bask in the glory of today. How good it is to be back in the swing of routines. Not that I haven't enjoyed the relaxed, easy pace of the summer. I have—every unexpected, unscheduled bit of it. It had a good and proper place in our yearly cycle. But I'm ready now for the predictable routines of the scheduled life that the school calendar imposes on us.

This morning I will make up schedules—daily, weekly, monthly. Block out upcoming events on my planning calendar. Then I will write up my lists of things to do. How I love my lists! Whether I actually do all those things really is beside the point. A deceptive (but wonderful) sense of control comes over me when I see my projects leaded into words; the exhilaration I receive from writing a list is second only to having in fact done those things.

I relish the comfortable ordinariness of the day and what it suggests to me of equilibrium, order, and a solid, dependable base of operation. If my rite of schedule making and list writing seems absurdly sacred, it must be understood it is one woman's attempt to steady one little boat amid the waves of distractions, demands, and multiplicity of choices. Ah yes, it is the *ordinary* that is extraordinary!

Back-to-school day. Red-letter day. You offer me a new chance to re-establish the hallowed ordinary. Certainly we need variety to add zest to the routine, but I for one speak in defense of the ordinary.

Now, on with the schedule, the lists, the planning calendar. Nursery school pickup will come all too soon. Then anything can happen!

HOME—FOR PEOPLE OR THINGS?

Crash! I rush into the kitchen just in time to see Jonathan fleeing from the scene. On the floor is my antique spool rack with the contents of its five shelves strewn across the room. Without bothering to determine guilt or innocence I chase after Jonathan and paddle him soundly on his diaper-cushioned bottom. Jonathan wails. I give him a piece of my mind. He shrieks.

"Hurt." He points to a three-day-old scratch on his arm in an attempt to divert me.

I pick him up, walk into the kitchen, and set him on a stool.

"Now you stay right there. I don't want you to move."

Jonathan has the good sense to obey me.

I lift the spool rack into its corner and then kneel down to assess the damages. One at a time I inspect the pewter plates and stack them on a shelf. Sugar covers everything. I brush off the cast-iron soup tureen and set it on another shelf.

"Sugar. Ucky." Jonathan tries to engage me in conversation. I ignore him.

I spot the top half of a candleholder. My heart sinks. Slate-gray pieces of pottery are strewn throughout the sugary debris. I pick up two pieces and try to fit them together.

"Broken." Jonathan shakes his head sadly.

This three-candle Mexican holder is beyond repair. It *belonged* on the top shelf of the corner rack along with the pewter sugar bowl and brownstone creamer. It may have been inexpensive but it was charming with its wired pottery attachments of leaves and birds. It can't be replaced.

I check out the antique creamer. Lift the hinged pewter lid. Undamaged.

"Good!" shouts Jonathan. I harden my heart against him.

A flat slice of blue and white china emerges through the sugar. I pick up the blue onion coffeepot. The lid has been chipped. As I slide the slice of china over the chip, another large nick comes into view. Futilely I sift through the sugar in search of the missing piece. The coffeepot could be replaced. But it won't be. It's just not necessary.

I wipe sugar off the remaining items—salt and pepper shakers, a miniature easel, a picture of a daisy-filled pot. The corners of the frame have been loosened.

Now in an all-time blue funk I sweep up the sugar. I suppress an urge to shake him. He watches as I move about the kitchen, cleaning up the breakfast dishes.

I mull over my tragedy. In a sense, I suppose I asked for it, leaving my treasures so blatantly on display. But what are my options? I could put them safely away. Yet long ago I determined to enjoy their beauty and take the risks. I could clamp down on the children. But this home is primarily for people, not for things. We have rules to cut down the risks but there is always this possibility. Accidents will happen. My possessions have their place—they are there to be appreciated, enjoyed, utilized. But once they begin to possess *me* they defeat that purpose. At least this is what I *believe*. But is this how I'm acting, withholding my love over an accident?

I glance over at Jonathan, still watching me, looking so forlorn. Removed from my circle of love. My broken treasures . . . What are they worth? Lovely to look at, invested with sentiment. Yes. But trinkets next to this little being—living, breathing, loving. Inanimate objects. A human life. How easy it is to get values turned upside down. Now is my opportunity to demonstrate what I really value.

I cross the room to Jonathan. "It's OK, Jonathan." He reaches out both arms. I hold him close.

Remember that the most important part of our happiness comes not from what we have but from how we live with those we love.

(Source Unknown)

31

THE DREARY ROUTINES

I'm so weary of all the small, insignificant details that make up such a large part of my life.

The dreary routines of housekeeping. Cooking food. Setting tables. Washing dishes. Putting them away, to take them out, to set the table. Over and over I repeat the steps until I can hardly discern a break in the cycle.

Picking up. I don't have a doubt in my mind that I could start at one end of the house and work my way through, then need to start all over again. And again. And again . . .

The floors always need sweeping. The fixtures scrubbing. The plants must be watered. Light bulbs replaced. Furniture dusted. Mirrors shined. Clothing washed. Pillows plumped.

It might help if there was applause when I finished dusting the last piece of furniture, cheers as I put the final dish away. But it would sustain me only for a moment. The fact remains, I have become so bogged down in the small parts of my responsibilities that I can't see how they fit into the whole scheme. The little things have become too big.

Pascal suggests there is a value in "the doing" that is independent of the specific task:

> Do the little things as though they were great, because of the majesty of Jesus Christ who does them in us and lives in our life. And do the greatest things as though they were little and easy, because of His omnipotence.[2]

No one can convince me that the act of scrubbing a floor is in and of itself a noble and lofty occupation. But I'm willing to consider that *how* I scrub that floor can carry greater significance than the particular job—that dignity can be invested in the task by the quality of workmanship and by the spirit in which it is performed.

Some work imparts an aura of greatness to the doer—other work becomes great by what the doer brings of himself to the task. The question becomes for me, is my task bigger than I or am I bigger than my task?

I refuse to be the victim of my own smallness. I will take these tasks, common and mundane as they may be, and invest in them a greatness "because of the majesty of Jesus Christ" who can do them in me and who lives in my life.

PRAYERS OF WOMEN (translated from the African dialect)

At the hour that I open the door of my house, I pray, my Lord, open the door of my heart that I might (be able) to meet with you!

At the time I wash my clothes, I pray, my Lord, cleanse my heart and cause it to be good and righteous that I might become pure white in your eyes.

At the time I sweep and clean around my house, I pray, my Lord, remove the trash and dirt that is inside my heart. Remove unclean thoughts that I may be thoroughly clean and pure in your sight.

When I go to buy oil, I pray, my Lord, give me wisdom—your wisdom, as the young virgins had as they had oil in their lamps. May I know and be ready at all times for your work.

When I receive a letter or when I send a letter to others, I pray, my Lord, enlarge my faith that I may fellowship with you, whom I do not see with my eyes, but whom I can know in my heart.

At the time I go to get water, I pray, my Lord, give me the water of life that I may never, never be again with thirst.

When I light the lamp, I pray, my Lord, let your true light shine in my heart. Help me that all of my affairs be with love, gentleness, and kindness, that my life may light that life of others in leading them to Jesus Christ.

When it is necessary to sprinkle water to the things I have planted I pray, my Lord, let the good rain of your Spirit fall on my heart.

When I boil the water to cook our food, I pray, my Lord, light your fire in my heart of coldness. Give me a strong yearning and desire in my heart to do your needy work with great joy. Amen.[3]

SOMETIMES GARDENER

What a day! A sudden cold snap has brought to the air an invigorating crispness. The early morning brilliance almost takes my breath away. I'm not alone in my joyous response. Crows, blue jays, cardinals sing in raucous exaltation!

I will celebrate this day by doing what I have put off so long—lawn work! I will make my peace with Mother Earth. The day commands it. I don my gardening garb and step buoyantly forth to greet the world.

Am I imagining, or do I hear green and growing things murmuring? Whispering about me behind their leafy cover. Laughing. "Do you see who I see?" "Well, look who's here! It's about time!" "Who does she think she is in that gardening getup?" "She means well," ventures a timid voice. "That's not enough." All manner of living things nod in agreement. "If only good intentions would a garden grow!"

I must stop my foolish imaginings. Defiantly I yank on my gardening gloves. I refuse to let guilt intimidate me. Someday I'll be on top of this situation. Have a gardening calendar. Fertilize, water, prune, according to schedule.

Now, on with the job! I set the children loose to pick up pieces of paper, large sticks and twigs. First the front lawn. I pull weeds. Cut back dead branches. Hoe. Rake. Fertilize. Give everything a hose-down. With professional deft I spray the roses. When did I last do that? Who knows? (Who cares!)

Buoyed by success I head to the back lawn. Dirt under the nails, pant legs rolled up, I'd pass for the real thing. I deliberate my plan of attack. With the innate good sense of a sometimes gardener, I make a quick judgment—keep it natural. Studied carelessness, it's called. It doesn't take long to create the desired effect!

I wind up my work by giving the sidewalk a vigorous sweep-down. The big finish! Then step back to survey the final results. Petunia-lined borders. Freshly turned earth. Red impatiens spill from the window box, gate basket, and randomly placed clay pots. The back yard is a profusion of color: white camellias, Florida holly, red blossoms dot the Turkish-cap border hedge. Tangerines and oranges are turning a vivid orange. Blue morning-glories shinny up a drainpipe.

Everything looks so groomed and tidy and neat. So right. I promise myself I'll never neglect the earth again. (Do I hear laughing?) For this estatic moment I'm totally at one with myself and with my world.

> *God's in His heaven—*
> *All's right with the world.*[4]

OH, FOR A GENTLE SPIRIT!

It's been one of those days. It started out so well. Maybe too well. This would be a stay-at-home day—I'd catch up on odd jobs I had put off for such a day as this.

I had such good intentions but everything is working together to foil my high resolves. Jonathan is underfoot. He insists on being held. The children's demands seem to be in direct proportion to my goals. I put off the children. "Not now. Mommy is busy." "Later." "David, see if Jonathan will drink some apple juice." "Can't you see I'm in the middle of cleaning these cupboards?" "Stop it, Jonathan! Put that down right now!" The children sense that my schedule has taken precedence over the rules; they push each rule to the limit.

I move into high gear. I am tense and tight inside. There is no "give." Words jump out too quickly. Much like a whirling dervish I spin about the house determined above all to check one more item off my list.

How I long for a gentle spirit! I want to be a calm in the center of the storm. Instead I *am* the storm. I begin to see the irony of my efforts to create an atmosphere of physical beauty at the cost of beauty of the spirit. Certainly my presence makes as tangible a contribution to the atmosphere of the home as does my cleaning, scrubbing, and polishing.

Getting things done. A gentle spirit. They are in conflict with each other. I seem to accomplish one or the other. But not both. When I am relaxed and easy, time slips away. Things go undone. When I set my mind to accomplish a project, everything becomes an interruption.

Yet if I strived to maintain a calm and gentle spirit as I went about my tasks, would my work really suffer? If I paused for a moment to look at a child as he talked, would he be so insistent in his demands? If I stopped everything to discipline firmly but lovingly a child who has stepped out of line, would he continue to push each rule to the limit? Getting things done. A gentle spirit. Are these two goals really diametrically opposed to each other? Or is the one, in fact, aided by the other? In my heart I hear the answer.

O God, how I long for a gentle spirit. Take my tension and strivings in exchange for your calm and peace. I know that a clean and orderly home would only be a mockery, if permeated by a spirit atmosphere that contradicts its physical beauty. Give me a gentle spirit, Father—fill me with your Spirit. Amen.

THE CLEAN HOUSE

The house is cleanly shining. Today I coupled my good intentions with action and subjected this home to spring housecleaning.

The children were distributed throughout the town (banished) to guarantee that this historic event would actually take place. How I cleaned! I pulled out furniture to sweep long-forgotten surfaces. Scrubbed baseboards. Washed fingerprints and nose smudges off windows. Dusted, vacuumed, polished.

Then came the final touches. I placed containers of greens and flowers in strategic locations. Finally I turned on crucial lamps to highlight The Results.

This home is as close as it will ever come to an ordered perfection. In the living room and dining room dark woods have been polished to a soft glow. Pale gold walls set off the jewel-like colors of the oriental-type carpets.

The kitchen is invitingly homey with its crisp blues and whites and pewter accents. Dutch clean! In the breakfast nook a drop-leaf table is backed up to the window at one end, its leaf extended on the other. It is flanked by high-backed church pews salvaged from George Whitfield's church in Newburyport, Massachusetts. On the homespun tablecloth, a delft-handled copper pot rubbed to a mellow shine bears a prolific ivy plant.

White wicker furniture and white ceiling-to-floor curtains crisply accent the jade-green walls of the master suite. The bedroom with its three walls of windows and the brass bed, spread with an English flower garden of quilted cotton, looks like a garden bower washed in early morning dew. On the bedside wicker desk is a tiny gallery of pictures. Clean, clean, clean.

Even the boys' room is an unprecedented clean! White walls, barn-red woodwork. Not a single wrinkle can be found on the denim bedspreads. Books are neatly lined up on the apple crate shelves; a pleasing clutter of toys decorates the room.

Kimberly's room looks like a delectable pink confection. Ruffled pink-and-white-striped priscilla curtains, held back by sparkling pressed glass disks, match pillowcases and freshly smoothed and tucked sheets. A room appropriately furnished in miniature for tiny doll inhabitants—four-poster bed, cradle, rocking chair, high chair, and stove. There are revealing evidences of mother-at-play: The tea table is set and four dolls sit engaged in polite conversation on pink eyelet-trimmed cushions.

Our home—shining, glowing, all in its proper place! I will celebrate these moments of perfection with a cup of tea enjoyed in leisure. Just me. In a spotlessly clean home.

I set a round silver tray with a silver teapot, footed tea strainer, cup and saucer of our finest porcelain, and a hand-embroidered organdy napkin. Now the final touch—a bud vase with a full-blown Tiffany rose. I pour boiling water over the loose tea leaves and carry the tray into the sitting room. All is ready! I step into the hallway and turn on the stereo. Handel, Mozart, and Beethoven each patiently awaits his turn to fill the house with his finest music.

Now! Slowly I drink the hot tea, savoring each herbal sip. The late afternoon sun filters through the sheer voile curtains illuminating the room with an other-world aura.

> O Lord, it's so lovely now, this minute, my house that I've just cleaned up. Thank you. Bless it.
>
> And bless me, too, as I stand full of love and sweet resolutions about keeping my house always so. Let me hold fast to the lovely image of order that will give way, all too soon, to the crumbs and trackings and chaos of living.
>
> Bless and fortify me against the times when there won't be flowers on the mantel or a fire on the grate, or shining silver and bathroom bowls. Let me store up moments like this, right now, to cancel out the crossness and impatience with such inevitable hours.
>
> Thank you, Lord, and keep guiding me back to them— these moments of perfection in my cleanly shining house. Amen.[5]

IS THERE ANY SAFE PLACE?

Dark, angry sky. Foreboding stillness. A deafening crash of thunder breaks the silence. Trees begin to bend and sway, assaulted by great gusts of wind. The sky opens aborting vats of water.

Outside—dark, wild, wet. Protected from the raging storm our home seems so secure. Nothing can touch us in this our safe place. Snug. Dry. Still.

The winds blow harder. The house trembles. Could the winds sweep under us and carry us away, helpless against their force? The lightning, at one with the thunder. Could we become its target? With one strike could we burst into fire and be devoured by hungry flames? What assurance do we have that the rising lake waters will be satisfied with their boundaries? What prevents them from a rebellious escape, washing us relentlessly in their current?

Do we deceive ourselves with our attempts at security? Do the elements wink as we build our protections? Bigger. Stronger. Do they mock us, knowing full well we are at their mercy? Are we poor deluded fools? Playing silly games—the odds against us. Should we settle with the elements? Show our cards. Admit we are no equal. Plead mercy. Impotent before wind, fire, and water. Vulnerable. Finite. Is there any real protection? Is there any safe place?

Wait. The winds are subsiding. Already lightning and thunder are separated by lengthening seconds. Raindrops now gently pit the newly formed pools of water. How quickly I lose my sense of perspective! This home has stood up to a half century of subtropical storms. And held its own. The winds bring refreshing coolness. The water, drink to a thirsty world. Fire, in subservience to man, performs all kinds of wonders. Day in, day out, the elements serve us well.

41

But before the unleashed fury of the elements, I stood humbled. The storm has given me this—"a proper estimate of my place in the scheme of things."[6]

I, for a moment, view things with this new sense of proportion. In what do I place my confidence? In edifices created by man, or in the Creator of man? "The name of the Lord is a strong tower; the righteous runneth into it and is safe."[7]

Most of the time I feel so secure within the four walls of this home, this place that shelters those people and things so close to my heart. That is how it should be. But when I demand from it guarantees for total protection, I have asked of it more than any earthly dwelling can offer. For at best, this temporary place we call home can only offer a foretaste of our eternal home—the ultimate safe place.

2

Memory Building

"Superimposed onto our routine pattern was the out-of-the-ordinary—the Very Special. You took these and turned them into events which instantly were declared Traditions. I feel you gave me the ability to cope with—even value— the ordinariness of life and the skill to create adventure out of the everyday resources around me."

LOSING HOURS TO KEEP THEM

On a whim we pack bag lunches, pick up some friends of the children, and head up to Mountain Lake Nature Sanctuary.

We lunch in a secluded picnic area. David buys peanuts for us to feed the squirrels. Kimberly buys her own with her "shoe money"—the reward for finding Jonathan's missing shoe. Squirrels come up and eat out of their hands; birds catch peanuts in the air.

Jonathan lags behind us, squatting to say "Hi" to each squirrel. "Hurry up, Jonathan," we call. "Bye-bye," he says to a squirrel.

They climb a hill and run down. Over and over.

"Last one to the car is a monkey's uncle!"

We sing all the way home.

A lost afternoon, one might say. Hours gone that could have been spent accomplishing something worthwhile. Edith Schaeffer views it from a different perspective:

> Remember that you are often choosing a memory. Many times you are not choosing what to do with the two or three hours for the immediate results, but you are choosing a memory (or choosing not to have that memory) for a lifetime . . . The memory multiplies the use of those hours into hundreds of hours!
>
> When you choose a memory in this way, you are choosing to lose hours of time—in order to keep them! A family should have a whole museum of memories gathered through the years—of moments when the choice has been to go ahead and lose a couple of hours in order to save them![1]

And what a welcomed dimension it adds to my life to be a fellow adventurer for an afternoon! Will the children remember our shared experience? Maybe not, but *I* will, and we all have benefited from it!

> *I meant to do my work today—*
> > *But a brown bird sang in the apple tree,*
> *And a butterfly flitted across the field,*
> > *And all the leaves were calling me.*
> *And the wind went sighing over the land,*
> > *Tossing the grasses to and fro,*
> *And a rainbow held out its shining hand—*
> > *So what could I do but laugh and go?*[2]

CHRISTMAS EVE REFLECTIONS

Christmas Eve! The house looks so lovely cast in the soft radiance of candlelight. I sink deep into the sofa and feast my soul on the festive beauty about me.

It's been such a busy day . . . Last-minute Christmas preparations—baking a pecan pie, making cranberry salad, wrapping gifts; the arrival of Grandpa and Grandma celebrated by a balloon-popping festival instigated by David; our candlelight communion service at church; the opening of presents around the tree (one at a time!), partaking of Christmas goodies wheeled on the teacart into the living room.

Opened presents and folded wrapping paper are piled under the tree. My gift to the family is not among the pleasing disarray; it could not be boxed and tied up in ribbon. It is a gift of the heart. A seasoned veteran of many holidays, I have come to terms with an indisputable law working in our activity-hungry society; if the family is not "scheduled into" the holidays, it will be "scheduled out" by default. So it was with loving determination I took my planning calendar, spread the month of December flat on the desk, and blocked out sacred family events and traditions. No detail was too small to be included. A family Christmas—my secret gift of love.

Decorating, Phase I of The Plan, was heralded by hanging the Advent calendar in its place of honor in the dining room. Christmas records were stacked on the stereo, the house was flooded with heart-bursting music. On the front door a swag of wheat tied in red plaid ribbon announced to the world the spirit of Christmas dwelt within! The house was gradually transformed with holly, ribbon, candles, and treasures from Christmas past . . .

46

The crèche—illuminated now by bayberry candles on the fireplace mantel—was our first serious project. Three little helpers stood on stools as I gently lifted exquisite hand-carved olivewood figures from light covers of tissue. The Christmas story unfolded before us as the manger scene was constructed—camels, three wisemen carrying gifts, shepherds, sheep and cows, Mary, Joseph, and finally the Christ child in a tiny manger.

Centered on the dining room table is our gingerbread house, a fantasy confection studded with candies and topped with a steep sloping roof swirled with white icing. The candelabra, bearing eight glowing candles, crowns our architectural triumph.

How we labored over the construction of this masterpiece! We mixed, baked, and cut out pieces according to pattern; parts were iced and carefully fitted on the gingerbread base; the roof was raised, decorative touches added. With a final dusting of powdered sugar our project was completed! Heart-warming affirmations were the dividends for this time-consuming undertaking; Kimberly, as the two of us unwrapped candies: "Aren't you glad it's just us!" David's astute observation: "The gingerbread house will be even better than last year—you get better all the time." (They forget so quickly!)

The Christmas tree fills its corner to overflowing—straight and tall, starred with tiny white lights, heavy with much-loved ornaments. This "just right" tree was the result of a two-day search led by tree expert Dave. A bird's nest, discovered deep within the boughs, confirmed this tree was intended for us alone.

Tree trimming occupied an important place on the calendar! One by one ornaments were removed from a box and laid on a tray, while the origin of each was reviewed. Children carefully delivered ornaments to Daddy, who spaced them on the tree. Jonathan's energy was sublimated through a drum ornament that set him off on a drum major routine—"boom, boom, boom, my little drum." When the last ornament was hung, we turned off the house lights and sat on the sofa to admire our dazzling creation, speechless for once—but not for long!

The children became wild with excitement; I turned into Scrooge and delivered an impassioned speech, "This should be a happy occasion for *all* of us, and frankly your screeching, running,

47

and poking make this home intolerable for *me. I'm a person too!*" I wound up my harangue by plopping all three in a tub of warm, sudsy water. Subdued children, looking innocent and cherubic in clean pajamas, joined me in front of the Christmas tree to read *The Night Before Christmas* enchantingly illustrated by Tasha Tudor. A shining moment.

The stage was set for Phase II—Christmas baking. With euphoric optimism groceries were purchased, recipe file purloined, and butter set out to soften. I woke up on the appointed morning with visions of Christmas cookies, gingerbread men, Russian teacakes, mints, and fudge. Jonathan woke up with a fever! As I sifted, stirred, and mixed, a whimpering little being in a white nightshirt clung to my legs. But I pushed on—wasn't it on the schedule? Nothing would comfort my suffering angel except my undivided attention. A war waged within: "I must keep on; after all, I'm doing it for him!" But I, like Cain, was laying down the wrong sacrifice; my offerings were meaningless in place of my attentions. A truce of spirit was declared. I settled Jonathan and myself on the sofa with pillows, blankets, current Christmas magazines, and a backup stack of past issues. Apart from a few telephone calls and light meal preparations, I was Jonathan's. He rewarded me with a soft song sung under his breath, "Mom-mee, mom-mee, mom-mee . . . ," the end syllable lifting into a high little chirp. All day long he gazed at me, occasionally reaching over to hold my hand. We communed at the deepest level. Merry Christmas, Jonathan.

The next day, both Dave and I awakened with sore throats. We limped along, trying to determine who was sicker. Dave won! So amid the administering of fluids and aspirin, I struggled with my attitude. "He may be sicker—but *I* still feel awful! When I determined to be a Christmas angel I didn't consider it might involve being a Christmas nurse, much less a *sick* Christmas nurse! What about The Plan? What about Phase II?" After several days of ambivalence (grudging service), I rose before the rest of the family and went to the corner restaurant to make peace with myself on neutral turf. A new Christmas angel returned to the "best nest"— halo adjusted, wings straightened, clutching onto a modified Christmas schedule.

48

Activities were canceled, baking and card writing were fit into salvageable chinks of time. Surprisingly, things *did* get done. Somehow, when Phase III rolled in, we were ready—sore throats reasonably under control—to participate in church and community activities. Pageant night when Kimberly and co-cherub floated down the center aisle, their halos skimming the tops of pews, and a white-robed David took his place in the Angel Choir, it was impossible to believe that sickness, weariness, and frustration were anything but the mental wanderings of a deluded housewife!

Here I sit with my musings, and there still is work to be done! I stand, walk to the fireplace to blow out the candles, and pause for a moment to look at the manger scene. A tiny carving holds my attention—the infant Jesus—visible reminder of God's imcomparable gift to man. A gift that cuts through all the traditions and celebrations in a Person and a Truth.

Such a gift demands a response . . . What can I give *Him?* It seems that a rightful response must be tied up in how I treat other people. Christ Himself taught us "the way we treat other people is the way we treat Him and is accepted as that."[3] (Inasmuch as ye have done it unto one of the least of these ye have done it unto me."[4]) How fragile was my gift to my family! How perilously threatened it was by The Schedule! How close I came to sacrificing them to the very things I was doing *for* them!

I'll go now, and fill the children's stockings with little gifts, tangible expressions of love. Tomorrow I'll work to carry off a joyous Christmas Day, intangible gift of love. All, in a sense, gifts to Christ. But I know at the bottom line there is only one gift I can give to Christ that is acceptable—and that is my life.

> *What can I give Him,*
> *Poor as I am?*
> *If I were a shepherd,*
> *I would give Him a lamb.*
> *If I were a Wise Man,*
> *I would do my part,*
> *But what can I give Him,*
> *Give my heart.*[5]

THE "OTHER PEOPLE"

What a crew! Grandpa, carrying Jonathan sling fashion in his arms, David walking alongside him, Kimberly skipping circles around them all. The very air is charged with excitement. Fearless four, headed for high adventure.

Later they'll return, proudly sporting hands stamped in green, proof that they were indeed at Cypress Gardens. This annual outing with Grandpa *is* a great treat, but I know if it was just a walk to the end of the block, Grandpa would turn even that into an adventure. *He* is an adventure!

Wistfully I see them off, wave them out of sight, thinking all the while of *my* childhood, heightened by Father's wonderful flair for creating something out of nothing. I think of the year when rising lake waters threatened to wash through our summer home. Worry was forgotten as we made sport of rowing to familiar landmarks in a sturdy little boat. Were we natives of Venice in exotic gondolas, or explorers sailing the wide-open seas?

That was the year of The Move. Construction of our new home was slow; we were forced to remain in our summer cottage long after school started, long after the bitter cold had settled in. What do you do when a summer resort town closes down for the season, when you've parted with old friends and haven't met your "future" yet? What do you do? You *create* an adventure! Father did just that. He spotted a "character" who looked remarkably out of place in such a forsaken town and led the family in serious sleuthing. Who was he? Why was he here? Where did he come from? I don't remember the answers to those questions (if, in fact, they ever were uncovered). I just remember days, weeks, even months of thrilling espionage: looking for our dashing hero;

finding him, say, in a coffee shop; casually walking in, sitting innocently in a booth across the room from him; casting covert glances as he made his way to his red Cadillac. Then the chase— oh, the chase! Racing to our car (allowing enough time to pass to allay suspicion), gaining on him, recklessly winding in and out of streets, until our mystery man would escape us once again.

A trip with Father to the grocery store held the promise of a purchase of chocolate-covered-marshmallow cookies and sneaking out two to eat on the return trip. Once home we would arrange the rest on a plate, then dispose of the wrappings. Did Mother ever know the package contained twelve (not ten!) cookies?

So it's with a strange little twist of the heart that I see them off . . . And rejoicing too, not only for "Mother's day off" but for that special something they will be receiving from their time with Grandpa, that undefinable "something" money cannot buy.

I rejoice too in the "other people" in our children's lives—the teachers, surrogate grandparents, family friends, the casual acquaintances who take a friendly interest in them; these people who enrich their lives with added experiences—a leisurely walk to the park, a trip to McDonald's, making paper dolls, playing catch in the back yard, a joint cookie-baking venture, dedicated instruction; the people who demonstrate extra-special qualities—patience, wisdom, unusual understanding, or a zany sense of humor.

It's reassuring to know there are other people who care. It takes the pressure off us to be everything, to provide everything for our children. The "other people" in their lives compensate for our limitations, complement our strengths, and remind us by their very presence we can't meet all our children's needs, nor do we have to—we're not alone!

VALENTINE PARTY

"Jonathan tried to eat chocolate hearts off the valentines!"

"But we wouldn't let him."

"He *did* tear the foil off one."

The children share their animated tale of delivering homemade valentines to our "neighbors" as they settle themselves around the dining room table. Dave, who accompanied them on their rounds, assures me that the cards did, in fact, make it to their destination safely.

"When do we get to open our gifts?" They are eying and fingering little packages wrapped in silver gift paper, "I love you" gifts —pure sentiment. Boxed heart-shaped soaps for the children (a loving reminder?), and a valentine candle for Dave—"you light up my life."

"You know. When we *always* open them—after dinner."

Admittedly, our family valentine party is the creation of a hopeless sentimentalist. China and silver and the faces of children are illuminated in the soft glow of candlelight. A silver Victorian cake basket bears several clusters of African violets fashioned into a nosegay of a sort. Pink place mats, pink napkins, pink heart-shaped mints in individual Haviland butter pats. Pink, pink, pink . . . even the valentine cake is pink!

Shamelessly romantic, I know. But it is my way of saying "I love you" to my family; of taking advantage of a traditional celebration and building from it a Family Occasion.

I'd only be fooling myself to deny I delight in every detail of our preparation; that this moment around the table is the highlight of my day. But I justify my excesses this way: It's so easy to take for granted those we love, to knock ourselves out for mere ac-

52

quaintances and walk right past those closest to our hearts in the assumption of our love. For this one day each year, at least, my family will be left with no question in their minds—I love them from the bottom of my heart!

BIKE HIKE

"Wait for us!" commands the Little Person strapped in the bike seat behind me. I pedal faster to catch up with the others—Dave and Kimberly, and David.

"*Here we is!*" announces Jonathan as we ease alongside Dave.

"Look at me—no hands." Kimberly spreads her arms wing fashion.

"Me too—no hands." For one half second, Jonathan releases his grip on the side railings. "Hi, duck," he congenially addresses a feathered friend waddling toward the bike path. "There's a boat! See!" He keeps up a running commentary on the sights and sounds along our lakeside trail.

What a day for a bike ride! Warm and sunny. Yellow butterflies skitter and glide on the breeze; white puffs of clouds are reflected in the deep blue of the water.

David falls behind, then pedals past us full speed. "I'm looking for an alligator."

"Twinkle, twinkle, little star," Jonathan breaks from his up-to-the-minute news flashes to burst into song. His voice bounces up and down with the bumps in the path.

Around the lake we pedal. Chatter. Stretches of silence. Finally we depart from the path for the upward ride home.

"I don't want to go home," Jonathan declares.

"Let's go to the Barrel," Kimberly suggests.

"Yeah, we *always* go to the Barrel after a bike ride," insists David.

Dave and I catch eyes. "We always do it this way" means: We did it once and liked it! "Do you have any money?" Dave nods in the affirmative.

So a thirsty five sit on swivel stools in the barrel-shaped A&W, sipping root beer from tall, frosty mugs, all because it's a *tradition* —tried once, fully approved, so decreed as such forever and ever, amen!

EASTER SUNRISE

4:45 A.M.! With merciless accuracy the alarm pierces our slumber. I slide deeper into the covers in an attempt to smother the harsh reality of awakening. Easter . . . Today is Easter! The sunrise service! There is much to be done in the next half hour!

Dave smuggles David past a slumbering Jonathan. "I've been awake since four."

"Kimberly, time to get up." Eyes open instantly, preconditioned by excitement to full wakefulness.

The children dress; I attend to last-minute details—turn over ham slices marinating in brown sugar, remove butter from the refrigerator, check the table setting in the dining room: white ironstone plates on yellow place mats, sunny napkins flared in pewter rings, tiny butter knives with a single flower painted on porcelain handles. I straighten a clay pot filled with yellow tulips—a purchase justified by a timely German proverb: "If thou art of all thy goods bereft and have but two loaves left, sell one, and with the dole buy hyacinths (or tulips!) to feed the soul."

Our baby-sitter arrives. David and Kimberly dance into the cool morning air heavy with the scent of orange blossoms. "It's *dark* out!" "Of course, silly. The sun's not up yet!" We're on our way!

Slowly we drive around the lake and proceed toward Bok Tower. I think back on all the planning and effort that went into this important family tradition. Preparations began two days ago with the baking of sweet rolls—an unalterable part of our established menu along with grilled ham steaks and honeydew melon garnished with fresh strawberries and grapes. Yesterday was devoted entirely to housecleaning, laundering, and yardwork. When the children were tucked in for the night I completed the

56

final projects—filling colorful Easter eggs with chocolate candies and jelly beans, setting the table for breakfast, laying out two sets of clothing for each child—warm pre-sunrise clothing and their Easter finery. Last night I asked myself, "Is it worth it?"; this morning I find my answer in the brightly shining eyes of the children, in Dave's buoyant spirit, in the joy breaking like dawn in my heart.

Throughout the service words of Scripture, song, and meditation proclaim the resurrection message. All of creation declares the same . . . The sun slowly rises; a new day awakens—"Now is Christ risen from the dead, and become the first fruits of them that slept. Hallelujah!" Earth sings her morning song; birds, squirrels, rustling leaves—"Let all things seen and unseen, their notes of gladness blend." Spring—new green, new life—" 'Tis the spring of souls today!" The Tower brasses cut through the air with a brilliance now matched by the wide-open morning sky.

We descend to our car and to an exceedingly busy day: an Easter egg hunt in the back yard, breakfast shared with friends, Sunday school, worship . . . The words of the anthem turn over in my mind; I determine to hold fast to the Easter message throughout the inevitably accelerating pace of the day.

GATEWAY TO ADVENTURE

There is no frigate like a book
To take us lands away . . .
Nor any coursers like a page
Of prancing poetry.

This traverse may the poorest take
Without oppress of toll.
How frugal is the chariot
That bears a human soul![6]

"Mr. and Mrs. Mallard were looking for a place to live." I read aloud from the children's picture book *Make Way for Ducklings.*[7] "But every time Mr. Mallard saw what looked like a nice place, Mrs. Mallard said it was no good."

The ducks' search for a satisfactory place to hatch ducklings leads them to Boston's Public Gardens. They take up with a large swan "pushing a boat full of people."

"Kimberly, Mommy and Uncle John actually rode on that swan boat when they were little," interrupts David.

"Is that true? Is there really a lake like that with swan boats?"

"Oh yes! Often we'd go to the Public Gardens on Sundays after church."

"Did you see these very things?" Kimberly points out park benches, fences, a large tree, buildings in the distance. "Were they there even when *you* were a little girl?" she asks, obviously impressed by their timelessness (or mine!). "Did you see Mr. and Mrs. Mallard?"

"Well . . . I did see some ducks, but I don't know if they were Mr. and Mrs. Mallard. I wouldn't be surprised, though, if we rode on that very swan boat."

58

Their sense of history satisfied, we read on: Bikes become a hazard so the ducks move on to a "nice quiet place" a little way from the Public Gardens. They build a nest and Mrs. Mallard dutifully lays eight eggs.

"One day the ducklings hatched out. First came Jack, then Kack, and then Lack, then Mack, and Nack and Ouach and Pack and Quack. Mr. and Mrs. Mallard were bursting with pride. It was a great responsibility taking care of so many ducklings, and it kept them very busy." About this time Mr. Mallard "decided he'd like to take a trip to see what the rest of the river was like, farther on. So off he set. 'I'll meet you in a week, in the Public Gardens,' he quacked over his shoulder. 'Take good care of the ducklings!'

" 'Don't you worry,' said Mrs. Mallard, 'I know all about bringing up children.' And she did."

Since Mrs. Mallard seemed to have such a positive attitude toward Mr. Mallard's timely exit, I refrain from making a verbal judgment on his character. Mrs. Mallard trains her babies well, and sets off with the eight ducklings in a straight line to make what proves to be a perilous journey back to the Public Gardens —across the Charles River, across the highway, down Mount Vernon Street, over to Charles Street. By the time they approach the corner of Beacon Street, four policemen arrive to hold back the traffic so "Mrs. Mallard and the ducklings could march across the street."

With the turn of each page, the children count off the ducklings, Jack, Kack, Lack, Mack, Nack, Ouach, Pack, and Quack. When they reach their destination "there was Mr. Mallard waiting for them, just as he had promised."

As I close the picture book I decide to let the written pages join hands with experience. "Who wants to go with me to the park and feed the ducks?"

Feeling much like Mrs. Mallard herself I lead my three little ducklings on a block-long excursion to the park. A duck and three fluffy ducklings swim to shore and waddle toward the children, who throw out pieces of bread. Suddenly they're surrounded with ducks arriving by air and water!

I watch as delighted children dole out crusts of bread to greedy ducks. Children who have been to Boston and back today; children who have traveled in time to my childhood—ridden the swan boat with my brother and me; glimpsed the marvels of the natural world—changing seasons, birthing habits of ducks; enjoyed a good plot sprinkled with humor, been exposed to the pleasure of well-chosen words, delighted in the rhyming repetition of the ducklings' names. How far they have traveled today! A shared adventure through the open pages of a good book! A book

introduces us to people and places we wouldn't ordinarily know. A good book is a magic gateway into a broader world of wonder, of beauty, of delight and adventure. Books are experiences that make us grow, that add something to our inner stature . . .

. . . a young child, a fresh uncluttered mind, a world before him—to what treasures will you lead him? With what will you furnish his spirit?[8]

FAMILY REUNION

Dusk. Lights from drifting boats dot the harbor. From my sea wall perch I watch day ease into night. Gulls swoop and soar. Waves crash the sea wall, spraying me with a mist of salt water. Nostalgia washes over me like the waters below as two weeks of family vacation draw to an end. Tomorrow we'll separate for another year—three families, three generations. Memories like waves roll in, crest, and break, washed over by other memories . . .

The children—brown, exuberant, glowing with health and the pure joy of living, exploring the dimensions of their special relationship—"cousins." In the pool, David, Carla, and Suzanne diving, swimming, performing greater and more daring acrobatics; Kimberly, gaining confidence, expanding her territory; Jonathan and Janet bobbing about in bright orange bubbles. The "big cousins" heading off to the game room; toddling babies imitating each feat of the other; Kimberly seeking to establish her "place"— mothering babies, being mothered by Suzanne, keeping up with the inseparable twosome, David and Carla. Children running the beach, playing tag with the waves, stopping to retrieve a shell, building castles, digging moats in the sand.

Grandparents—bestowing gifts of love, handing out bouquets of praise. "Suzanne! Aren't you afraid going off that high dive?" "Look at Carla—she's like a fish. Yes, yes, you too, Kimberly!" "You don't mean to say you made the hole in four strokes, David!" Babies preen and strut, reaching heights of achievement spurred on by grandparents who have never seen such beautiful, clever, and precocious young! Each child in his turn heading off with a suitcase to spend the night "all by myself" with Grandpa and Grandma; returning with bags of popcorn "to share," homemade cookies, perhaps, and the general sense of well-being from having been singled out for special attention.

Twelve people in various combination. Dave and I, John and Anne dressing up, leaving the children, going to the hotel for an elegant evening buffet. The poolside chats. Walks to the lighthouse, hand in hand with Dave. Brothers-in-law drawn into the mystic fraternity of Golf. Mothers comparing notes on child rearing and life situations. Stolen moments—rising before the others, heading off with a good book to the coffee shop for Danish; walking the beach, alone.

The family powwows—the active dynamics of three generations. Children bedded down; adult discussions. Grilling one person. Coming on too strong, backing off. Focusing on another. Reflecting on values, childhood conflicts, adult responsibilities. Stretching, growing, within the loving challenge of unconditional acceptance. Twelve people, in vital relationship—touching base, going separate ways, bringing out various facets of each person.

For this, and more, three families plan, sometimes sacrifice, each year. And yearly, too, Dave and I question, "Should we spend the money? Think of what we could buy with the money we'd save—carpeting, new upholstery for the sofa, ten speed bikes, a stereo, or a grandfather clock."

A vacation vs. something "concrete," something "permanent" —how does one weigh such things? How does one compare their value? Take the things we'd like to have; choose one, choose two, take them all and put them on one side of the scale. Now add vacation benefits to the other side: relaxation, recreation, renewal. Easy now, the scale is in balance. Add the stretching, challenging conversations, insights from the exchange of generations. Ah, the scale is tilted. Growing relationships, loving support. Weighted to the bottom, scales reversed.

How quickly "things" take their place alongside other accumulations and fade into the whole. But two weeks removed from routine pressures, nourished by supportive relationships, stand out like a brilliant jewel to be savored, cherished, and drawn upon for the remaining fifty weeks of the year!

A BANK OF MEMORIES

"Mommy, will you read to Kimberly about the time I threw cereal on the floor?" David comes into the kitchen with a beseeching look on his face. Kimberly follows, tagging at his heels.

Hesitating only for a moment, I lay down my dishcloth and walk to the dining room. From the cabinet I pull two clothbound notebooks, turn a few pages in search of the "cereal story," and begin reading:

> I walk into the kitchen just in time to see cereal flying in every direction. The floor is covered with Cheerios. David, perched on his high chair, is wearing an expression of pure delight. He has a backup fistful of cereal.
> "No, no, David! We do *not* throw cereal on the floor!"
> "Mommy! David does *not* throw cereal on the floor. He throws it up in the sky!"

The children howl with laughter! Silently I read on. This incident is followed by some of David's questions and observations about the coming of the "new baby."

"Listen to what David said *after* you were born, Kimberly."

> "Do you wonder why God gave us Kimber, now that she's turned out to be so naughty? Don't you wish you could put her back into your tummy again?"

By now I'm hooked. We move into the living room and sit down. I read aloud:

> David: "When I bend over like this (he bends forward from his waist) why don't my eyes fall out?"
> Kimberly: "Our lawn needs a haircut."

Kimberly: (while we stand waiting by our grocery cart for someone to clean up the yogurt Jonathan tossed overboard) "Do you sometimes wish we weren't us?"

David and Kimberly giggle—older, wiser, beyond such foolishness. I'd forgotten these comments. I wonder what things are lost forever because I failed to write them down?

"Oh, listen to what David did when he got a new bank for his birthday!"

David walks into the living room carrying his new bank and shows it to a friend who is visiting with me.

"David," she asks, pouring a purseful of change into her hand, "how do you like pennies?"

Eying her open hand sparkling with quarters, dimes, and nickels, he answers firmly, "Not very much!"

"What did the lady do?"

"Much to my embarrassment she gave you some nickels, dimes, and quarters. *After* that, you decided you'd take some pennies too!"

I scan the pages, selecting incidents to read aloud. "Well, that's about it. I'd better get back to work. And it is long past your nap time." David and Kimberly grin at each other like little conspirators. "Run along now!"

In addition to the sheer pleasure of reliving moments from our shared past, other benefits are emerging from our growing collection of memories: diaries, family memory book, baby books, photo albums, and the verbal reliving of an experience— "remember when . . ."

It is not just memories we are building, but family unity, a spirit of togetherness. They become a reminder that we belong to each other, that our happiness is in some way tied up in each other.

A feeling of worth is imparted to each family member as his or her value is demonstrated through carefully kept records and memorabilia. Each picture, each written moment, each shared experience says to the possessor, "You are important—you are a special person."

A remarkable sense of perspective comes from the keeping of memories. We can look back and see how we survived a difficult period of time, be buoyed by a happy incident, find the inspiration to create new memories. Things take on new significance when seen as part of the span of a lifetime.

Through the years we are investing in a bank of memories to be drawn upon for the rest of our lives. As we savor a special moment in leisure, hopefully it will be etched more deeply on our consciousness. Who knows when we will need it? To tide us over a long separation; to comfort us through a time of emotional drought; to hold before us an ideal of what a really good time can be. Who knows when it will be all we'll have of each other?

I close now. The dirty dishes still await me in the kitchen. I've lost the better part of an hour. But the time was not wasted!

SENTIMENTAL JOURNEY

Lunch has been served. Kimberly is taking her "play nap" in her room; Jonathan has finally fallen asleep in spite of great resistance. I have exactly forty-five minutes before I must pick up David from school. This is my own special time, daily anticipated, though not always realized. I sit down with a book saved for this very moment. In my line of vision is my round table crowded with memorabilia lovingly chosen for this place of importance. The cleaning of this dust-laden clutter is inevitably ruled by circumstances—the arrival of company; the sweep of routine housecleaning. Bone-weary, I can actually feel energy surge through me as I am carried with the force of a preposterous idea. I will take these precious minutes of mine and invest them in an absurd luxury—the leisurely and sentimental cleaning of my table. I will dust and polish and shine, slowly and deliberately. I will linger over "the chosen" that represent memories so dear as to be set aside in this special place. Quickly but carefully I clear the table, setting each treasure on the nearby wicker sofa.

I scrub off the dust and some water rings from the table top now enameled white. But I'm back in New England at Longfellow's Wayside Inn. Across the street is an auction. Newlyweds on a seminarian's budget are fools to go near such places. We cross the street. For an unchallenged four dollars we buy two round tables. Back in our apartment we are hilarious with delight —such shrewd and canny buyers!

Now I wetly wipe the lid of a wedgwood box given to me as a bridesmaid's gift. Judy was one of the first of our friends to get married, finishing up college in three years to our four. Idealistic and dreamy, we were a bit in awe of her, daring to march out

66

ahead of us into unknown territories. (I just received a letter from her with a picture of her two children enclosed and an announcement of a third to come.) I laugh when I think of my attempt to enshrine her face forever in a plaster of Paris mold for an art class project. Unfortunately, for lovers of beauty everywhere, the project was never completed due to her inability to keep a straight face. Old friends; such good friends.

New friends are dear friends too. I pick up a little heart-shaped container formed in porcelain. I rub it firmly and the tiny rosebud delicately painted on its lid stands out in detail. Pennie was there when I needed her. With uncertainty I awaited the arrival of my first baby. Her husband delivered that baby and she, a three-time mother, showed me how to care for him. Between feedings and demands of young children, we snatched moments to talk. I shared with her how Mother often marked a special occasion with the gift of a delicate box, and one day she arrived on my doorstep with this heart. It is hinged and inside is a waxy perfume which I've never worn. (I cannot help but notice it has been rubbed into tiny finger grooves by little people who must have opened this container again and again unbeknown to me.)

I pick up another heart-shaped box. Mother brought it from Vienna years ago. I see into the golden cagelike box to the lining of green velvet. My mind drifts back to my sophomore year of high school. I was wearing a dress of this green velvet and awaiting almost with panic my first date with a boy I had secretly admired for over three years. We went to an elegant restaurant for dinner and I hardly could eat a bite on account of my highly charged emotional state! (I remember rearranging food on my plate to appear like less, hoping he would not suspect.) Now, most gingerly I dust the hinged glass lid so as not to rub off the forget-me-nots painted in oils. No, I've not forgotten that childhood sweetheart of mine—I married him some seven years after that fateful date!

The porcelain box from Tiffany's—what a go-round Mother and I had over that item. She encouraged me to buy these as presents for my bridesmaids in our wedding. I insisted on buying beaded loose powder compacts. Now that I think of it, not one of those girls used loose powder! But I did establish myself as an independent thinker. And Mother ended up buying a porcelain box for me. What busy days those were—winding up my student teaching and college studies and shaping plans for the wedding. One day I would have happily walked out of my childhood home without a second thought; the next day I wanted to stay safely home forever.

I pluck a few dead leaves from the potted Swedish ivy set in an open latticed vase. On the rim are hand-shaped grapes and leaves of white glazed pottery. This was one of my first wedding gifts—from our across-the-street neighbors. Mrs. Paine opened her house to us neighborhood children for lessons in crafts. I still have somewhere cards of flowers made from tiny colored seashells—one of our artistic triumphs. Their children married, they moved away, we've lost touch.

Now I begin the glass shining of picture frames. What loving energy Grandma Bricker put into the selection of gifts for her ever increasing family. Together we settled on this "just right" frame of gold filigree. Centered at the very top of the frame is an enameled inset of roses. Several pictures have passed through the frame, but the frame has held no other occupant since the day we slipped Kimberly's one-year-old picture into this, its rightful place. Her golden hair all fluffed around her serious little face, she is clutching onto her doll, Peter. (I had other ideas for the name of her first doll, but she and Daddy named "her" before I had my chance.)

Grandmother Bricker. She lived ninety-one remarkable years. Images of Grandma flash through my mind . . . White-haired and stiff with arthritis, she is faithfully counting out her daily exercises; she is in the kitchen going through her morning wheat-grinding ritual, preparing the grain to be cooked into hot cereal, nutty-flavored and nutritious; I see her face, washed in abandoned delight as she listens to us recall our day: "No, you don't mean it!" she interjects, or "You don't say!"; she is sitting on the sofa absorbed in the reading of her well-worn Bible, dictionary at her side to supplement her sixth-grade education.

Smilingly, I remember the mouse incident. My friend was spending the summer with us. A mouse scurried into our room and darted under the bed; we jumped on the bed and squealed for help. Grandma came, sized up the situation, and disappeared. Soon she returned with a broom in her hand, saying with absolute sincerity, "Lord, we've got a mouse to kill." How consistent that response was to her whole life! Energetic, vital, and openhearted, she was the great affirmer in my life. Even as people, places, and events became age-blurred in her mind, she maintained a true sweetness of spirit.

Kimberly's personality is best captured in a tiny mosaic frame now in my hand. Then two, she was kneeling in unmown grass, completely absorbed in some small study of her own. Her yellow dress was covered with an eyelet pinafore, her hair pulled into two ponytails clasped in satin ribbons. Abstract and subtle, it looks like a Renoir painting, a portrait in miniature.

Setting this down, I pick up one more picture. I look into David's eyes—so wise and all-knowing. It brings an almost physical tug to my heart to realize how fast this seven-year-old child is growing, how old he is becoming. I compare this picture with his one-year-old likeness in the oval frame. It could pass for Jonathan! We must get a picture of Jonathan—poor third child.

I polish another frame—a silver one—and lay it flat on the table. The rose velvet ribbon is fading. It doesn't seem that long ago we vacationed at the ocean. I held closely David and Kimberly, vacation-tanned with hair sun-bleached—a matched set. I can at will calm my spirit by fastening my thoughts on restful vacation days. They represent not only memories of past joy, but the promise of respite again when we will pack up and leave behind routine pressures in exchange for special, leisure-packed weeks.

Finally, I blow the dust from the bone china flowers on my Staffordshire vase. Roses, forget-me-nots, pansies. I'll never forget the day I bought this extravagance. I had a small sum of money in my purse; I was undecided as to what necessity I would cross off the ever growing list—shoes, underwear, extra groceries. Without determining that, I boldly walked into a favorite store, seized this vase, and laid my money across the counter before I could change my mind. I may always feel just a little bit guilty about that dramatic act, but it represented something very important to me. In the midst of days of busy service to children, home responsibilities, and other demands, I stopped for a moment to consider myself, to

69

enshrine in this object the thought "I'm special too." It wasn't conscious, but was it mere coincidence that I chose one more box, a symbol in days past of a marked occasion or simply a gift from the heart?

Now I arrange each treasure in its assigned place. I adjust a box, straighten a frame only seconds before the buzzer rings (previously agreed-on signal of the end to Kimberly's nap). With one lingering glance, I view with deepest satisfaction my work—shining, glowing cleanly, each in its proper place. By nightfall things will be rearranged by little hands, crumbs may fall on one or more of the treasures.

Kimberly bounces into the room. We shall awaken Jonathan and, together, pick up David. My spirit is renewed and my heart is singing. Memories are dear, but *now* is priceless!

3

True Creativity

"You felt a child's play was his 'work' and toys were the 'equipment' and you chose carefully the few toys we owned. We, too, took them seriously and they opened all kinds of avenues for creative expression. You provided opportunities for us that were the testing grounds for interests. These opportunities had their cost and, I know, involved definite sacrifices from you, but how they enriched my life."

WHAT IS CREATIVITY?

Coloring books, playpens, and the traditional classroom stifle creativity. Or so we're told. On the other hand, Montessori methods, Creative Playthings, and the unstructured classroom promote it. Of course, it's not as simple as all that, but messages bear down on us just the same, and we are left with a sense of confusion. What seemed "acceptable" at first may not be after all. We might "produce" a well-behaved child at the cost of stifled creativity.

Then we meet Johnny (supposedly a creative wonder) and are repelled by what appears, to our untrained eye, to be obnoxious behavior. Do I want my child to be like this? Because of the emphasis today on creativity, I'm forced to ask some questions. What is creativity? Why is it important? How do I go about eliciting creativity from my child?

While the word "creativity" connotes different things to different people, certain gifts and abilities are generally accepted as "creative." If we limit ourselves to any concept unofficially sanctioned by our society or subculture, we might be in danger of molding our children into a "creative conformity."

I see God's view of creativity as being open-ended, unique, individual. Are we not creative beings made in the image of our Creator? There is biblical evidence that God has formed us, writing a plan or design into our very beings. It should then follow that we could reach our fullest creative potential by discovering that plan and putting it into action. A plan found within our person, an unearthing of that which has already been implanted by our Creator.

True creativity seems related more to the discovery, development, and actualization of God-implanted seeds than to a creative act or work. These seeds may grow into something which defies our preconceived notions of creativity; it is even possible we might appear to be creative without having begun to touch on our true creativity.

I can't *produce* creativity in my child. I can only nourish those seeds planted deep within him. My job is that of an enabler—I may provide a broad exposure to a variety of experiences, and make available the tools to put his leanings into action; I may take his efforts seriously by being sensitive at the right moment to give encouragement, direction, or diversion. But then I must stand back and observe . . . listen . . . I must be careful not to read into him my dreams but must be alert to those things that reveal his dream. Paul Tournier says, "It is a violation of the person of the child to try to direct him in everything according to what his parents think best, without heeding his own preferences."[1] He will never realize his full potential except through the utilization of his own innate gifts.

What an awesome task—the calling forth of gifts! It is fraught with complications. Yet as a parent I am in the enviable position of being able to observe in my children the early indications of their creative bent before it is stifled by outside influences.

I realize my influence on them is limited; in terms of their lifetime, my input is minimal. Of greatest importance, then, is to imprint into their minds the understandings that can free them to discover their true selves. A lifelong process. One that will be facilitated by an adherence to this crucial scriptural principle:

> Be not conformed to this world: but be ye transformed by the renewing of your mind, that ye may prove what is that good, and acceptable, and perfect, will of God.[2]

I'M SOMETHING SPECIAL

Kimberly and I sit on the wicker sofa watching the Muppets on television. Kermit the Frog sings, "It's not easy being green." He goes on to reflect that "brighter colors make a bigger impression; green simply blends in with ordinary things." Kimberly looks up at me with concern. "Mommy, if I were a frog, I wouldn't mind being green."

"Why?"

"Because I'd be happy just the way God made me."

Kimberly, in childish simplicity, touched on an understanding basic to a healthy self-concept; God forms each individual with a unique design and purpose.

> *For thou didst form my inward parts;*
> *Thou didst weave me in my mother's womb.*
> *I will give thanks to Thee, for I am fearfully*
> *   and wonderfully made;*
> *Wonderful are Thy works,*
> *And my soul knows it very well.*
> *My frame was not hidden from Thee,*
> *When I was made in secret,*
> *And skillfully wrought in the depths of the earth.*
> *Thine eyes have seen my unformed substances;*
> *And in Thy book they were all written,*
> *The days that were ordained for me,*
> *When as yet there was not one of them.*[3]

This understanding is beyond Kimberly's grasp. Yet, with the trust of a four-year-old, she unquestioningly accepts her God-given uniqueness. So far there has been nothing in her relatively uncomplicated existence which has put her self-acceptance to the test. When asked, "Who in the whole world would you most like to be?" she answers without hesitation, "Me!" It's easy for Kimberly to supply the answer to Kermit the Frog's problem of low self-esteem with, "I'll be happy just the way God made me." She's perfectly satisfied with the way *she* is! Up to this point our input has gone a long way toward meeting her basic needs. We, her parents, are present to help her over the rough spots—"Only babies bring dolls to show and tell." "I've decided to invite someone else to my house today."

But during the process of living, her worth inevitably will be challenged. She will face rejection, people more gifted than herself, personal limitations, defeat. It is essential that she learn to base her worth on something stronger than the human props on which we all rely so heavily. Her self-image will be profoundly affected if she *really* believes she was designed by God. This belief will influence the way she regards her strengths; it will likewise make it easier to accept her limitations.

There is a song we discuss and sing:

> *I'm something special, I'm the only one of my kind,*
> *God gave me a body and a bright healthy mind,*
> *He has a special purpose that He wanted me to find,*
> *That's why I'm something special, I'm the only one of*
> *my kind.*[4]

I hope, as she sings these words, the sense of her God-given uniqueness will be etched onto her mind. I pray she will know, no matter what happens, since God made her, that she *is* something special.

STOCKING THE CHILD'S WORKSHOP

"It's my turn to have the castle today." With that David drops the Fisher-Price castle on the sitting room floor and begins his work. Horse-drawn coaches, drawbridges, secret stairways, lookout towers, dragons, dungeons, knights, kings and queens on royal thrones are the stuff of which his intricate plot is woven. I watch as David is transported to a faraway world of splendor and adventure.

Serious business, this matter of play. Before my eyes the castle is transformed from "just a toy" to something of great importance: a tool to implement a child's play toward creativity.

Am I giving a child's toy too much importance? Not when it is seen as a part of a bigger picture: as one of the many things which make up the raw materials for a child's "work." Nor can I take too seriously the way in which I "stock" the workshop of my child's experience. I approach it with a merry seriousness, attempting to provide a balance of "materials" for a wide range of exploration. His is a liberal education through play—he can specialize later.

Gradually we are building an arsenal of equipment, durable and open-ended in function—recreational, tools to explore the natural world, water gear, games and puzzles, art supplies, books, records, toys, props for make-believe—an investment of a sort that began with the first rattle, grew with the first child, expanded to meet the needs of more children, and includes a waiting list for "someday." Some of this equipment is the result of careful budgeting; most bears minimal monetary value, some no cost at all. My job is to assemble the materials, suggest or demonstrate their possibilities, provide accessible storage, and walk away . . .

I'm learning not to be discouraged by a child's near-predictable response to new "materials"—a strong initial interest followed by abandonment—since usually, in his own time and in his own way, he rediscovers them and claims them for his own. If this is slow in coming I might try to rekindle his interest by relocating the "investment" more prominently or by showing a low-key interest in it: "I wonder how you get these 'wheels' on the sticks." This, of course, is his cue to say, "I'll show you how" and take off on his own. But if his final response is "Read the directions," I must conclude it just might not be for him!

It is intriguing to see how one child's interest can trigger response from the others. Jonathan's discovery of an abandoned baby doll tossed carelessly into a stroller became a gold mine for him. He removed supplies from a diaper bag, one at a time, and applied their proper function to poor baby; bent over the stroller, body hunched in concentration, he sprinkled powder, smoothed it with a little pink puff, dispensed medicine through a bottle (patting baby comfortingly all the while), brushed her hair, methodically replaced each item, then wheeled the stroller around the room twice and started all over again. He repeated these steps until Kimberly, a knock-down-drag-out later, usurped the parent role. David appeared on the scene and under his skilled direction their play reached its most sophisticated form—characters were reassigned, action defined.

Paul Tournier suggests, "A child's games are a better indication than his schoolwork of what he will do when he is grown-up. The child who can play well will also do well in his career . . ."[5] Sometimes I'm farsighted enough to see how a child's play fits into the total scheme, but mostly I delight in the immediate benefits: children absorbed in play; happy, untroubled hours in a fantasy world limited only by the boundary of their imaginations.

> *The work of water is bubbles!*
> *Day is the job of sun.*
> *Green is the business of gardens,*
> *and the duty of children*
> *is fun!*[6]

NOTHING TO DO

The children are underfoot in the house. I encourage them to go outside and play.

"Why don't you go bike-riding?"

"No."

"How about practicing hula-hoops?"

"No."

"OK," I announce, "let's *all* go out. No one will be allowed in the house until four o'clock." It's three thirty-five—I think I can make it.

We stumble out into the Florida heat. To think it is only the second day of summer! I toss a ball to David. He unenthusiastically throws it to Kimberly. It hits her. She screams. I keep trying. I hang a hula hoop on a limb of a grapefruit tree, then throw a ball through the hoop. The idea takes hold. Jonathan's eyes light up. Quickly I hang another hoop on a limb and put another ball in his hands.

At last I can sit back on a deck chair and watch the children play. "Nothing to do," they say, and in that pronouncement is the hint of a dare—"just see if you can get me interested in something!" When they are in that frame of mind I can suggest one activity after another to no avail. But when I join them myself, and *get them started*, it's predictable—before long they are totally absorbed in their play and more than happy to carry on by themselves.

Mother's Proverb: If a job started is a job half done,
Then getting play started is a battle
half won!

COMMAND PERFORMANCE

"See! My picture!" Jonathan, wide-eyed with amazement, points upward as I hang his first "work" along with David's and Kimberly's in the "gallery" on the hallway wall.

He watched with interest as I placed a white heart, stamped with his wee handprint and bright red paint, on red and white polka-dot paper; he stood fascinated as I wove red satin ribbon through an eyelet-bordered ruffle and glued it carefully around the heart; he was right at my side as I set his lovely valentine in a black frame. But not until now has he fully comprehended that *his* "picture" has reached the pinnacle in our hierarchy of display!

The screening process is progressively selective: All artwork is instantly displayed on the refrigerator door, regardless of artistic merit; in time it is moved to less prominent display on the hall bulletin board; finally (unclaimed or forgotten) it is inconspicuously transferred to its final resting place—wastebasket or scrapbook—as determined by Mother, resident art critic. But every so often (joy of joys!) a "masterpiece" is selected to be set in a gaily painted dimestore frame and hung for posterity. Da Vinci's, Monet's, or Renoir's greatest work could never inspire the awe-struck appreciation written across the faces of children who look up at pictures thus labeled: STUDY IN CIRCLES—DAVID—AGE 3; APPLEPRINTS—KIMBERLY—AGE 4 . . .

Children love an appreciative audience. Don't we all! The family, as a "birthplace of creativity," is not just for children. "The family should be the birthplace of the wife's creativity and the husband's creativity, encouraged by each other, by the children as they get old enough to encourage their parents, by sisters and brothers, aunts and uncles."[7] To this day, an accomplishment has not come full circle for me until shared with Dave or my parents. In the face of unsullied affirmation Dave will ask, "What do you *really* think?" Inevitably Dave and I are called in to witness a perfected puppet show, little chairs lined in a row for the audience; a "happy face" on a school paper well done is brought to the attention of the family; already Jonathan punctuates each accomplishment with "Watch! Watch! Watch meeee!"; a call can be heard from the back yard, "See how many times I can jump on the pogo stick." We have come to understand the term "command performance" to mean—you watch, while I perform!

> Creativity needs the availability of reaching the attention of a sympathetic friend at just the right moment. This is true in budding of creativity in an early childhood moment, but it is just as true in the serious creativity of a genius. Someone needs to come and watch, listen, look, respond . . .
> . . . The need for sharing what is exciting in bringing this forth—whatever this is—needs response. The spark must meet another spark, or the fire dies out and dark discouragement can flood in.[8]

How easy it is to discourage another with well-meaning advice or critical overtones—even laughter. No age is immune to this. When Jonathan made his first appearance in "real boy underpants" (bought to encourage potty training) he stepped forth self-consciously, saying, "Don't laugh, it's not funny."

Being supportive and encouraging requires a conscious sensitivity—listening as a child shares the seeds of a project, aspiration, dream or voices an accomplishment (or discouragement); providing materials or assistance when needed. Sometimes it demands simply the good sense to know when to give the child (or adult) the space and freedom to be alone. I'll never forget the sandbox incident! Dave stood at a window and watched a two-year-old's intrinsic motivation killed by my steady stream of praise. As little David became increasingly "hooked" on my heady words of admiration, he became less and less interested in the pure joy of building sand castles.

Are we being overly indulgent if we involve ourselves in each other's accomplishments and pursuits? No! We not only love an audience but *need* one!

STRUCTURING TIME ALONE

Play-nap time! I make a quick check to see that all is under control.

Kimberly's room has been transformed into a schoolhouse. Dolls wait patiently on chairs pulled up to a table while "teacher" distributes supplies from her special bag—colored pencils, paper, scissors, erasers.

In the middle of the sitting room floor lies David, flat on his back. His index fingers are engaged in animated dialogue. Back and forth they converse, David's voice changing with the shift of characters. Who knows what fantasy is being enacted with his simple props!

There is no doubt about it—their one-and-a-half-hour play-nap is a precious block of time in my day! I guard it, anticipate it, then relish my solitude. And this time structured for aloneness is no less valuable for the children. Even at best they can get too much of each other. Time apart eases tensions; at the end of their legislated separation they bound to greet each other. It offers a space of time to assimilate the previous happenings of the day, make plans for the hours ahead—or simply do nothing at all.

Limited to one room, they must create their own entertainment from the available materials. As the play-nap forces them to draw upon their inner reserves, it becomes, in a sense, a time block for resourcefulness. Here play reaches its most sophisticated level— out come games, toys, and puzzles which are often ignored when pitted against more stimulating options; materials are put together in unique and complex combination (necessity truly *is* the mother of invention!).

Never have I had a single qualm about imposing this daily confinement on the children since I know it provides for them something they need but themselves would not elect—time to be alone.

ENERGY CRISIS

Dark, rainy, late afternoon. Pent-up, keyed-up children. Crisis—a surplus of energy and no way to expend it!

"Run get your rhythm instruments." I select a record with a strong march tempo. Three noisy children return: clash, clack, bang, and shake! Cymbals, clappers, and tambourine in deafening outbursts. David thrusts a tone block into my hand. "For you!"

"Get ready." I lower the needle to the first band of the record and adjust the volume. Instinctively they fall in line and begin to mark time.

"Now!" March. March. March, march, march. Down the hallway through the kitchen, into the dining room, around the table. Knees high, beating time, in perfect step with the music. Into the living room, Kimberly's room, through the passageway, out to David's room, back into the hallway. March. March. March, march, march.

We take our turn as leader. David. Kimberly. At last Jonathan —around and around the dining room table we follow his dizzying lead. Clearly expendable, I slip away.

They march in increasingly intricate formation—in and out of rooms, around furniture, never missing a beat. Finally, exhausted, they flop on the living room sofa, energy spent. Crisis resolved.

A PLACE OF ONE'S OWN

"Once upon a time there was a little girl who wanted a playhouse all her own." The children settle in on either side of me on the porch swing, as we wind down for bedtime. "On the corner of her lawn were three evergreen trees with just enough room inside to set up housekeeping. Limbs for cupboards, branches to hang things from—it transformed into a snugly efficient abode. She played in her house every day. Then winter came and filled it with snow. She moved indoors to the attic, but was gradually crowded out by boxes.

"That summer she occupied a little lattice porch at a lake home. She moved in her possessions—an apple crate for kitchen supplies, table and chairs, trunks and suitcases filled with doll clothes. Perhaps the finest feature of the home was the swinging door with a real latch! What a grand dwelling place! But people would stop and watch; some would ask questions. The lack of privacy forced her to move again.

"Then she discovered the Perfect Place. Over the garage was a loft that could be reached only by a ladder. It was deserted, private, and secure. Never had she enjoyed so much room! Here she even had a "desk" and chair and writing supplies. A beam lamp provided the necessary light. Could one ask for more? Day after day she played in her lovely, lofty home—until she fell out! It resulted from a slight error in judgment; it would surely never happen again—but her parents unreasonably said she could no longer play there.

"She read books about *real* playhouses—how she envied the girls of the *Dandelion Cottage*; she imagined herself one of the family of the *Boxcar Children*. She loved to walk by a certain house that had an old 'milk-truck playhouse' in its back yard. But she had to content herself with inferior, temporary dwellings.

"She grew up and got married and had children of her own. Now everyone knows that grown-ups don't have playhouses. Well, that is *most* grown-ups—for if you were to visit this girl-who-grew-up today you would see that she is the exception. You could see her playhouse—gray with white trim, it has windows and shutters and its very own window box. A little bench sits on the front porch just inviting friends to come and chat. And the door is painted bright red."

"Mommy?" David breaks his faraway gaze to look up at me. "Was that little girl you?"

"Yes . . ."

"But you *still* don't have a playhouse. It's really our house. Right, Mommy?" insists Kimberly.

Yes, it's really *their* house, but when that little house was positioned in our back yard, something deep inside me was satisfied. Something even bigger than the realization of a childhood dream. It satisfied a desire of mine for *our* children—to have a place all their own.

It is their territory to do with as they please. A place to act out their dreams—today a castle, tomorrow the cabin of an adventure-seeking ship. Child size, they fill it, dominate it like no room proportioned for adult purposes. It is there to receive them when they are hurt or angry and need to work out something away from observing eyes. A meeting place for friends. Or just what it appears to be: a little house to enact their emerging concept of the adult world—"I'll be the mommy."

So I consciously restrain myself from carpeting, wallpapering, and curtaining their house. I'll stick to mine, and let them shape that house with their schemes and dreams.

PRODUCTION

Labor Day. Dave takes off for an eight-thirty "meeting" on the green!

Anticipating a long day I pull out A Dozen Little Plays[9] from my "emergency kit." Together we leaf through the pages till we reach full agreement on a selection—*The Giant's Cat.*

Out comes the folding table. Kimberly and David round up scissors, string, Magic Markers, staplers, and paper bags. Kimberly colors and cuts out a cat mask. David designs a donkey head from a large paper bag. I work on a rooster crown and mouse ears. Jonathan "helps" everyone.

Costuming complete, we settle down to our "script." There is some discussion about how to handle the dialogue. We decide to ad-lib our lines, saving the giant's part for Daddy.

Dave's return is greeted by wildly excited children. He rehearses his lines: "GET OUT OF MY WAY, EVERYBODY!" (In the darkness the animals unite and "make like" a giant.) "HOW STRONG THE GIANT IS! HE IS TOO MUCH OF A GIANT FOR ME!" (Giant retreats, tricked by barnyard animals.)

His lines are under control. We make a quick adjustment in the script (Jonathan's asleep). The play begins.

> CAST: Giant—Daddy
> Cat—Kimberly
> Donkey—David
> Rooster—Mother
> Sleeping mouse—Jonathan

The performance comes off without a hitch—and without an audience. Everyone takes a bow. Curtain.

All in all, a most productive day!

85

NO TIME FOR KIMBERLY

David is at school; a restless Kimberly clamors for my attention. I resolve to set aside some time this morning just for her.

The morning runs away from me . . . Jonathan fusses; I work to divert him. A friend stops by with a bag of "just picked" tomatoes and we talk over the porch railing. I grab a moment to plan the day in my calendar, finish off a letter for today's mail. Jonathan must be settled for a nap. The morning is almost over—I must set out my four-day-old zinnia seedlings while Jonathan is still asleep. But there is no time for Kimberly.

After a moment's mental debate, my "better self" wins and I call, "Kimberly, come help me with these plants."

She pats the soil after me, chattering all the while.

"Aren't I a big help, Mommy?"

We move on to the next task—scrubbing furniture in the playhouse. Kimberly glues a broken chair. Now she joins me in the screenporch, 409 in one hand, wet rag in the other. She scrubs an end table. There is a comfortable sense of togetherness as we work, Kimberly commenting on her every move. I doubt that a "planned activity" would have brought her any greater enjoyment.

This shouldn't come as a surprise when I consider how much of her play is spent in imitation of adult work. She fusses over her baby Susie, repeating words of advice with a most familiar intonation. When I write, she settles in beside me with a pencil and paper, producing hieroglyphics that bring her great satisfaction. On her trike, she heads to the "grocery store," verbally figuring out her list. My "tea parties" can't compare with hers. How she fusses! With tiny dishes, she spreads a feast that is equaled only by a full-course banquet. But when I say, "Kimberly, come help Mommy . . . ," she drops everything. To work with adult materials is the ultimate of child play!

This seems to bear out the importance of simply *including* children in daily routines. The perfect activity, planned and designed especially for the child, is a rare event. Everything works against it. But to include a child as one works—handing him a broom, a dustcloth, a cup of sugar to add to the batter—while not practical in every situation is certainly a realistic possibility.

It does slow me down. It is inconvenient at times. But what a small price to pay for the camaraderie found in working together! And from our joint efforts, experiences are stored up to be drawn upon for "variations on the theme" in their own imaginative play.

WHAT IS RED?

Red is a sunset
Blazely and bright
Red is feeling brave
With all your might.
Red is a sunburn
Spot on your nose,
Sometimes red
Is a red, red rose.
Red squiggles out
When you cut your hand.
Red is a brick and
A rubber band.
Red is a hotness
You get inside
When you're embarrassed
And want to hide.
Fire-cracker, fire-engine
Fire-flicker red—
And when you're angry
Red runs through your head.
Red is an Indian,
A Valentine heart,
The trimming on
A circus cart.
Red is lipstick,
Red is a shout,
Red is a signal
That says: "watch out!"

> Red is the giant-est
> Color of all
> Red is a show-off
> No doubt about it—
> But can you imagine
> Living without it?[10]

The children sit quietly on stools and eat peanut butter and jelly sandwiches as I read from *Hailstones and Halibut Bones*, a book exploring the dimensions of color.

"Red is a stop sign," adds David.

"And Jonathan's bike," chimes in Kimberly.

On they continue, trying to outdo each other with images of red—apples, wagon, a mean feeling, "my favorite color," measles . . .

Inspired by their responsiveness, I decide to complete the circle of their experience. I set up an easel in the kitchen; tape large sheets of white newsprint on either side; distribute paintbrushes and bottles of red paint purchased for just such an occasion.

"I want to paint, too." Jonathan appears from nowhere. I tear off an extra sheet for Jonathan and lay it flat on the kitchen table.

They dip bushy brushes into little pots of bright red paint—thick, smooth, "mud-luscious." At first they hesitantly venture timid dabs of color on the white expanse before them. As images take form, they become less inhibited. Soon all caution is thrown to the wind; with reckless abandon they sweep wide strokes of paint across the paper. "Look at my apple." Jonathan points out blobs of red. "Here and here and here." "I'm doing good on my balloons!" "That gives *me* an idea." "Would you untape it? I want to start another one." "Oh no! I dropped my brush!" "Oh no! Me too!" (Jonathan deliberately drops his brush, and smears more paint on the table in his attempt to "clean up.") "Hey, look at my valentine heart!" "Let me see. . . ."

Helplessly I watch as our carefully structured activity spins totally out of my control. Red is everywhere! Smudged across radiant faces, spotted on clothing, splattered across the floor, dribbling down the wooden legs of the easel . . . Red is feeling out of control!

Feebly I exhort, "Do try to be careful." But I know full well it is not only an impossibility for them to heed my admonition, it is a necessity for them to make a mess.

What happens when *I* tackle a writing project? Out come fresh paper piled high in a box, sharpened pencils, books and notes on a particular line of thought. I spread my tools around me. Ready now! Completed work is stacked to my left; rejected scribblings are tossed freely over my shoulder, putting to death once and for all unacceptable material. What does the kitchen look like when I'm rolling out dough for sweet rolls? Pots, pans, and bowls clutter counter tops; open jars, open canisters, open cupboards are visible through a cloud of flour. The liberty to create and a neat home are at opposite extremes of the pole; creativity demands the freedom to make a mess.

So I throw out a stop sign on my feelings of red and add one more response to the question "What is red?": Red is the freedom to make a mess!

SPECIALIZATION

T-ball. David's first brush with organized sports. He stands on the pitcher's mound looking so little, so unsure. The ball rolls by him. He runs after it, scoops it into his glove, then looks around, uncertain where to throw it.

All my ambivalence toward organized sports rises to the surface. Is he too young? Is the competition healthy at this age? Does this force a child to "specialize" when he should be free to "meander" and explore?

My questions are in vain; it's gone beyond all that. T-ball is in David's heart and mind. It possesses his entire being. The moment he arrives home from school he bats a ball around the back yard; he walks through the house pounding a ball into his mitt; he puts on his oversized baseball cap, gazes in the mirror: "I'm the kind of guy that looks good in big hats."

But more valid than either David's feelings or mine is the objective recognition that T-ball has initiated a legitimate new stage for David—the beginning of specialization, the developing of skills. Not only is it satisfying to a child to acquire proficiency in a given area, but it is essential to his self-esteem to have skills to fall back on when the going gets rough.

Dr. James Dobson says, "Compensation is a child's best weapon against inferiority."[11] He expands on the importance of developing compensatory skills in his book *Hide or Seek:*

> I recommend that you, his parent, make a careful assessment of his areas of strength. Then select a skill where you believe the greatest possibilities for success lie. Once this selection is made, see to it that he gets through the first stage. Reward him, push him, threaten him, beg him—bribe him, if neces-

sary, but make him learn it. If you discover later that you've made a mistake, back up and start over on something else. But don't let inertia keep you from teaching something emotionally useful to your offspring! Does this form of coercion infringe upon the freedom of the child to choose for himself? Perhaps, but so does making him eat properly, keep himself clean, and go to bed at a reasonable hour. It is, as they say, in the child's best interest.[12]

Baseball may be only a passing fancy, a happy pastime. He may never make the big leagues. Who knows what avenues he will travel before he finds satisfying "compensatory skills"? Sports, music, natural science, mechanics, art, history . . . Who knows? But I do know it is not too early for David to begin developing some areas of strength by acquiring knowledge, by mastering new skills.

So go ahead David, play your game, dream your dreams. It is a part of your coming of age—and a part of *my* coming of age as well!

AN EVENT

Early morning. Fog covers the earth like a woolly blanket. The children discover the opaque whiteness with awe: "Where have the houses gone?" "You can't even see the street!"

I pull from the bookshelf our *Golden Treasury of Poetry:*

> *The fog comes*
> *on little cat feet.*
>
> *It sits looking*
> *over harbor and city*
> *on silent haunches*
> *and then moves on.*[13]

We become the fog, creeping on all fours without a sound; silently ("ssh") we approach the "harbor and city" and rise to our "silent haunches" for a moment, and then move on. Again and again we repeat our three-part drama, softly whispering the script as we move through each scene.

Our act comes to a hilarious end when Jonathan with whole-souled earnestness begins to whisper, "Ribet, ribet, ribet," obviously mistaking the word "fog" for "frog"!

Adventure with no cost, an attitude really. Seizing the potential of the moment, and turning it into an event.

THE ROUNDED LIFE

"*Pleeease* let me help!" Kimberly watches longingly as I fashion a baby card from doilies, lace, and ribbons.

"Why don't you go and play? I have to do this by myself."

"Just let me paste the bow on. This would be a good spot." David places a gritty finger on the pale pink of the card. I silently (and grimly) count to ten.

They stand on either side of me, wrapped in the spell of the flotsam and jetsam spread in tantalizing array on the dining room table. Frustrated by their closeness and permanence, I acquiesce to the pressure of the moment and scout around for a piece of poster board. I gather up the scraps, and turn the children loose with paste and scissors.

They cut and paste, conferring with each other about the placement of their designs, and I continue my work. Gradually they fill their "canvas"—cutouts from silver and gold foil doilies stand in dazzling relief against the royal blue background; bits of satin ribbon, colorful shapes from gift paper help craft their collage.

Now these two blond heads are bent in deep concentration—I can so clearly see the role adult example plays in triggering creativity in the child. Had I suggested the same activity for them to do by themselves, it is doubtful they would have responded. But catching me in action, possibilities began to turn over in their minds; they began to itch to hold the scissors in *their* hands.

The challenge for Dave and me is to live fully rounded lives that touch and explore the rich opportunities life has to offer. We can plan some of these experiences for our children. But, better yet, we can live them ourselves and include the children when it is appropriate or reasonable and fitting.

94

Does the specialization of our times work against the balance that once came from the natural passage of living, I wonder? What was a necessity—baking bread, planting a garden, putting up preserves, weaving cloth, sewing clothing—is now a commodity. Thus, exposure to a wide range of creative skills, which might have been a routine part of our parents' heritage, must be for us and our children personal choices. We cannot go back in time and re-create that need, but we can take from the present what is good and attempt to generate what is lacking. Just as I can choose not to weave and sew, I likewise have the freedom to choose endeavors I consider worthy of my effort and time.

So I speak for the rounded life—filled with a variety of pursuits that both renew and energize the person. It is healthy and good. And when I become caught up in Routine-and-Responsibility and foolishly regard the creative processes as personal indulgence, I must remember I am not the only one to be considered; the children, too, will profit from exposure to my wider set of interests.

WALKING WITH JONATHAN

"C'mon, c'mon! Outside! Outside!" Jonathan's vocabulary built from one and one half years of experience can be remarkably precise when it is expedient to him. He grabs onto my finger and makes lunging movements toward the front door. I try to divert him.

"Jonathan! See the ball. Let's play catch. Quick, get the ball, Jonathan!" I inject a quality of excitement into my voice which sounds irresistible to me. "Get the ball!"

"C'mon! Outside. Outside." He is pulling me in earnest now. Diversionary tactics are out of the question. A gasping sound accompanies each tug. He looks up at me with an expression akin to that of desperation. "Outside, Outs-i-i-de!"

I try my "limited logic line." Kneeling down I look him straight in the eyes. "Jonathan, honey, Mommy's busy. We can't go outside now." My voice is soft and soothing. I make my appeal gently. "I've got a *good* idea." I stand up with the intention of guiding him in the general direction of my "good idea." "We can play with the castle and the people."

He compromises one step toward my direction, then stops and looks deep into my eyes. You can feel the tension of this moment as his will hangs in delicate balance. A smile breaks over his face. Dimples appear. The corners of his eyes crinkle. Standing straighter now he takes my other hand in his. He is winsome. Charming.

"Mommeee," he says patiently, as if to one slow of understanding. "Mommy," he continues in a tone that suggests "you may not understand now but you'll appreciate this someday," "C'mon. Outside. Walk."

He doesn't need to plead. Tugging is unnecessary. He is totally confident I have accepted that this is simply one of those things— we are going on a walk! Releasing one hand he leads me toward the door. I turn the knob and pull the door open.

"Car! Car!" he shouts, pointing toward the street. I sense he is determined to make this a positive experience for me. He allows me to help him down the steps. He turns around, waves, and says an emphatic "bye-bye" to the house. Grasping my finger more tightly he steers me to the right. He is fully in command. We step from the shade of a tree into the bright sunlight. "Hot," he states, as his bare feet make their first contact with the sun-baked pavement. A car passes us. "Hi, car." Jonathan cheerfully continues to extend himself in friendliness to each passing car, not discouraged by the lack of response.

Suddenly he drops my finger and points to his shadow which precedes him. "What's that?" He stoops down and touches it. Stands up and runs, fascinated by its constancy.

A blue jay flies into his line of vision. "Bird, bird!" he calls, making the r whirl in his mouth. The blue jay comes to a landing by a bush near the sidewalk. Jonathan's off and running, arms outstretched, calling, "Bird, bird." The bird hops to the next bush. The chase is on. Bush to bush hop-flies the jay, unconsciously tantalizing Jonathan, who almost makes it each time. I end the chase by grabbing Jonathan around the waist. All the while he is kicking and screaming, "Bird, bird, bird, bird . . ." If given a proper chance, he certainly would have caught that bird!

I set him upright on the sidewalk again. His squealing protest comes to a halt when he spots a hole in the pavement. He kneels down and inserts his index finger into the hole, testing its depth and diameter. He traces a crack that extends from the hole with his other finger. An ant crawls into the scene.

"Bug!"

"That's an ant, Jonathan."

"An ant," he repeats. "An ant, an ant. An ant."

Now he spots another ant. And another. He squeals with excitement and crawls after one.

Without warning he abruptly stands up and continues walking. "C'mon," he says, looking back with a what-have-you-been-waiting-for expression on his face. Suddenly I feel foolish kneeling on the sidewalk of Central Avenue, midday, looking at ants!

He walks onto the lawn, drops to all fours, and rubs his hands through the grass. Then he pulls one blade of grass from the ground. He is now an explorer making an important discovery. What is this green stuff so cool and soft? Pull it. It breaks away. Touch it and it folds over. It doesn't taste good. For a moment I see that blade of grass through Jonathan's eyes. I feel his wonderment. And mourn the loss of childlikeness in the adult.

But wait! I, too, am possessed of wonder. No, I don't pick up a blade of grass and turn it over and over. I see it from a different perspective. Yet, I do wonder at the greenness of this grass, which was so stiff and brown before last week's rain. Spots which were bare have been filled in as the grass took over. And I know with certainty that wherever it has rained, this same transformation has taken place. And I stop to wonder at such predictability and the Mind that ordered it so. Oh yes . . . I wonder. But not with the wonder of a year-and-a-half-old baby. One is not superior to the other, but each unique to itself. We can learn from each other, but we should not imitate.

Jonathan tests his observation—soft to touch, subject to him, not good to eat. Again and again he will put his observations to the test until one day he will cease to wonder. He will know. But there will be something else to capture the mind of this wee explorer. And again, he will wonder . . .

His study has come to an end. Grass is flying in every direction. I appropriately choose this moment to set his course homeward. In the exhilaration of the "now" he appears unaware of this shift of direction. Body bent slightly forward, both pointer fingers extended, he is geared toward discovery. "What's that? What's that?" he commands as we continue walking. We're making some time now. He comes to a complete halt, points to the sky, and shouts, "Boat! Boat!" "That's right, Jonathan. There's a plane!" He grins over at me. "Right. Plane."

He slaps his arms to his side and heads up a driveway. When he reaches the top of the incline he turns. With his body thrown slightly backward, he runs full speed down the driveway singing, "Wheeeee." His chubby little jowls bounce each time he makes contact with the pavement. There could be no end to this. "C'mon, Jonathan. Let's go," I urge as he begins up the driveway again. I am amazed when he co-operates. But not for long. He has spotted another driveway and is headed toward it. By the time I have caught up with him he is coming down for the second time. "Wheeeeee."

He kicks a pebble, looks around, and discovers there is a pebble-filled strip the entire length of the driveway. He is ecstatic. He jumps in it, pokes around a bit, then starts winging pebbles one at a time as far as he can. "No! No!" He is sobered by the urgency in my voice. Immediately he starts retrieving pebbles one at a time and replacing them in the strip. This could take all day. Methodically he continues. This calls for an abortive effort on my part. I swoop down and remove him bodily from his work, my hands clasped under the full length of his body, his arms and legs flailing in protest. He calms when I set him down two lawns away from those pebbles. Faster than lightning he turns and runs back to the pebbles.

"Jonathan, come right back here!"

Stooping down he guiltily grabs a handful of pebbles.

"Jonathan!"

He pretends not to hear me. But I have my I'm-going-to-have-to-spank-you voice. Jonathan recognizes it. He stands up, pulls open his jeans pocket with one hand, and slides his handful of pebbles carefully into the pocket. Then, with dignity, he makes his way slowly and deliberately toward me. Every movement he makes shouts "I am doing this of my own free will. I have left the pebbles because I chose to, not because you said so." The pebbles-in-the-pocket routine was mainly face-saving. I'm willing to compromise. I don't mention the pebble-filled pocket. Our unspoken truce is sealed by his grabbing hold of my finger and walking companionably at my side.

Our home comes into view. Dropping my finger, Jonathan breaks into a full run much like a horse returning to the stable. I look at that little person running his bow-legged fastest—his patched dungarees held up with a leather belt; his white T-shirt. His deep summer tan is contrasted against a halo of sun-bleached hair. Such a little man! For all the world I would gather him up like the baby he really is and hold him tightly to me. But I won't. It would be disrespectful. Not now . . . Instead I savor the gradually diminishing sight before me.

Yes, Jonathan dear. You were right. There really wasn't anything we could have done this morning that could have begun to compare with going on a walk with you!

LEARNING TO SEE

Golden rain trees. Proudly they guard our front walk, bearing their upright torches of gold.

People are divided on their opinion of this tree. "It's a mess," some say. They're right. But *what* a mess! The golden torches will soon send their drizzle of blossoms to carpet our sidewalk. In their place will be fragile parchment-like bubbles of pink. It will be the glory of our street! Not even the block-long canopy of oaks can compare to its magnificence. Granted, this moment is short-lived, followed by the shedding of pods, then sticks, and finally leaves. Yet, when these trees stand embarrassingly naked amid lush subtropical foliage, I will already be anticipating their upcoming season, when they will again come into their own.

The golden rain tree's brief season of beauty may be its "reason to be." But as far as I'm concerned, if its only contribution was to stand there and shed, that would fully justify its existence. For when the brilliant umbrellas of pink begin to fade, the trees are just coming into their own for our children. These two trees shower my three little collectors with a wealth of treasures.

The "collecting season" begins with the seed pods. Out come their buckets. They pile the pods rim-high and empty them into the wheelbarrow. Before they weary of this daily activity, round dark balls emerge from these delicate receptacles. Now the challenge is filling an entire bucket with seeds. It has never been done —a bucket tips over, the children become sidetracked. But they always come back to it. The seeds have an irresistible pull—until the twig stage. Slim, pencil-straight twigs drop to the ground. The idea is to collect handfuls of sticks and stack them in neat bundles on the front porch. Here they remain to be drawn upon until, their possibilities clearly exhausted, they are abandoned.

The whole miracle of life is in panorama before the children in these trees. As they experience so intimately the wonders of the natural world, I pray that they will learn to see from the creation, the Creator.

> Ever since God created the World, His invisible qualities, both His eternal power and His divine nature, have been clearly seen. Men can perceive them in the things that God has made.[14]

God's invisible qualities are clearly demonstrated in His Creation. But it is my responsibility to assist my children in this discovery. When I observe how man takes from the Creation without considering the Giver, how man worships the Creation instead of the Creator, I cannot assume that my children will see. I must give witness to God's power in the phenomena of life. How He sustains all life in rhythmic flux—birth, fulfillment of its unique purpose, end, and new beginning. I must point out how God's divine nature is reflected in His Creation. Creative. Beautiful. Orderly. Predictable.

As I guide them in seeing, I pray that they will learn to see. I pray that they will come to a personal understanding of the Creation-Creator relationship as they see God's principles manifested in the natural world. For they will reach their fullest creative potential as they come to a pragmatic understanding of this truth: True creativity comes into being when the Creation is at one with its Creator.

4

The Shaping of Character

"Your real emphasis was on the development of character. There was never a question in my mind that the inner I mattered far more than anything I could achieve or accomplish. You saw *life* as the real arena for character development, and you dealt with each situation as it presented itself. You took our problems, conflicts, and wrongdoings as the stuff out of which characters are shaped."

AT WHAT PRICE, PEACE?

Church nursery. Three little toddlers standing in a row, hammering wooden pegs into holes in separate benches. Tat, tat, tat. Merry elves about their busy work. Jonathan lays down his hammer and goes to check out the scene in the "housekeeping corner." Another child lays down her hammer, replacing it with Jonathan's discarded one.

"Mine!" A bloodcurdling scream punctures the air. Jonathan whirls around and grabs onto his hammer. "Mine! Mine! Mine! Mine!"

"No! It's mine!" bellows the other child.

Deadlock. Adult mediation is required. In an all-out effort to restore peace I appeal to the little pinafored angel. "Why don't you give the hammer to Jonathan, honey?"

She looks at me as if I'm out of my mind. With authority based on a child's sense of fair play she insists, "It's mine."

She's right. Jonathan abandoned his claim to the hammer when he set it down. That is the unwritten but fully understood rule of church nursery. Why then have I sided with Jonathan? Because of a conditioned response based on my desire for peace at any cost: Give in to Jonathan so everything will be all right again. I'm stunned by this revelation brought about by the drama before me —two little people white-knuckle-clutching the wooden hammer, screaming in unison "mine, mine, mine . . ."

I pry Jonathan's fingers from their death grip. He searches my face for an explanation for this betrayal. Then falls flat on the floor with great weeping and gnashing of teeth. Self-righteously Toddler ✳2 resumes her hammering. Within sixty seconds, Jonathan arises, lifts his arms up to me for a hug, then takes the other hammer and positions himself companionably at her side.

How many times a day do I adjust the circumstance for Jonathan to avoid conflict? "David, just *give* him your truck. He'll get tired of it in a minute." "Let Jonathan go first—he's only a baby." "Don't take that book from Jonathan! You *know* what will happen. Now leave him alone." "He didn't mean to hurt you. Stop your crying, and act your age!" How many times a day have David's and Kimberly's rights been violated to preserve peace?

It all seems so clear, here in church nursery. It's not good for him; it's not fair to others. But the issues become blurred when I'm trying to prepare a meal, practice the harp. Consumed by accomplishing a goal or meeting a deadline, I have habitually put peace above more important considerations.

Blessed youngest child. I'm told you will take the world in stride. You have known nothing but the hilarious adoration of older siblings; basked in the full enjoyment of adults made confident by two go-rounds of parenting. What a good way to be initiated into the world! May I not be guilty of abusing your "head start" by making expediency my guide. May I, instead, build on my growing security in mothering, that I will not fail you where it really counts—in the shaping of your character.

THE EXPERTS—WHOM CAN I TRUST?

The experts . . . It was the "experts" who told our parents to adhere to a strict infant feeding schedule; to toilet train at an early age; to tell their children to "do what I say just because I say it." It is the "experts" who have told us that babies function better on a self-demand feeding schedule; early toilet training can lead to neurosis; adult directives suppress a child's spontaneous spirit. Now I discover these polarized viewpoints have been lumped together and called "traditional." What is their common denominator? They are *child*-centered. A new breed has emerged, reflecting the current advice of the "experts." In contrast to the traditional, the new breed is *self*-oriented. They are encouraged to give up nothing for their children, and to demand nothing in return.

The experts . . . They speak with authority; set forth logical theories; present convincing care studies. Whom can I trust? Do I embrace #1 on the best-seller list, then abandon it for its replacement? Do I rigidly adhere to the familiar—it worked for *my* parents? Choose the theory that supports the way I do things? Or sort through their collective counsel—picking and choosing, my judgment the measure? I don't want to cut myself off from sound advice, new insights, practical methods. Neither do I want to be blown to and fro, carried on the breeze of each new theory. How do I sort through their conflicting messages? What is my measure?

If I believe the Scriptures to be true, anything that contradicts biblical truth is false. The teachings of the Bible must be my measure of truth. I must back up the advice of the experts to the Bible and submit it to this test: Is it consistent with scriptural principles? Where it is in agreement, I am free to embrace it. Where it is in conflict, I must reject it.

What *does* the Bible say about the nature of the child? He is foolish and in need of limits and correction.[1] What does it say about parents? They are the God-designated authority for children.[2] The Bible affirms the psychological understandings about the basic need of man for love, security, and worth, and has established the family as the place of nourishment and nurture. I am compelled as a Christian to line up *all* the input I receive—secular *and* religious—and test it against these concepts. What I learn about my parental responsibilities gives me the confidence to assume my legitimate authority. What I learn about the emotional needs of my child checks me from abusing that authority.

I *am* thankful for the experts.* They have put me at ease about night crying, shyness, and several other difficult stages. With their combined assistance we've worked through a severe eating problem in one child and come up with creative play suggestions for three active children. With their charts they have settled it once and for all—our children *are* normal.

Oh yes, I'm thankful for the experts. But most of all I'm thankful for The Expert who gave me the Scriptures as an anchor to secure myself to, as I freely explore the contribution of the experts.

---

* My standby is a Zondervan publication, *Help! I'm a Parent,* by Bruce Narramore. It is a basic textbook on child rearing that has an accompanying workbook to aid in applying general concepts to the specifics of one's own situation. Dr. Narramore is qualified by training and experience in the field of child psychology and writes from a Christian perspective. His practical advice, delivered with humor and realism, reflects his own position as a parent of young children.

THE GOAL OF DISCIPLINE

"YOU CAN GO RIGHT TO YOUR ROOM, YOUNG MAN, AND DON'T COME OUT UNTIL I TELL YOU!!!" With a push and a shove, David is off to his room, in disgrace. My words ring in my ears.

David has been "at" Kimberly again, pushing her to the limit with his relentless put-downs. Much to his dismay, I walked into the room while he was right in the act of grinding his heel into the open wound. I had no choice but to step in.

There is no doubt that David was in the wrong. We've been through this many times before. He knows better. It is not only my right but my responsibility to deal with his behavior. Why then do I feel so bad?

I guess in my heart, I feel I've mishandled the situation. He has been punished, put in solitary confinement. Certainly punishment has a legitimate place, but in this case I complicated matters with my anger. Even if anger were not a factor, I'm only too aware effective discipline should involve a positive side. I'm left with the unsettling question, "What has David learned from the whole incident?" I've let him know his behavior was unacceptable. But have I taught him a better way of behaving? Have I put into his heart a desire to do the right things? If the purpose of discipline is to promote growth toward maturity, then not much has been accomplished.

I recall a conversation between David and me a couple of weeks ago. David came into the kitchen while I was mixing biscuits.

"Yesterday I was as good as I ever could be."

"At school?"

"Not just school. All day long. At home too."

"I did notice how good you were, David. It was fun having you around. I was even able to take a nap while you all watched 'Sesame Street.' I really believe I have you to thank for that."

"I know. I'm the oldest. Usually when Kimberly and Jonathan get screaming, I have something to do with it."

After I recover from my shock at his astonishing candor I ask, "How do you explain your good behavior?"

"Well, the night before—after I was tucked in—I decided I was going to try to be good the *whole* next day."

I'll never know what preceded his decision to behave. He may not know himself. But I do know there was nothing in my handling of this occurrence that would have put in his heart the same desire. Is it too late to redeem the situation? What tactic could I take now? I mull over my options . . .[3]

Communication. What *more* can I say? It is not as if he doesn't know how I feel about his put-downs. He could probably repeat my opinion on the subject verbatim!

Positive reinforcement. Just tell me one positive thing I could reinforce? Too late for that! There is nothing positive to build on in that tyrannical shake-up.

Natural consequences. The only *natural* consequence of his behavior is Kimberly's bloodcurdling screams. He seems to delight in them! No, *that's* no help.

Logical consequences. Perhaps this is it. David is a logical little guy. He can be reasoned with, and he takes like a man his just due if he understands exactly what is behind our action. His banishment was a kind of logical consequence for his disagreeable behavior—it may not be too late to explain that in a way that can appeal to his basic good sense.

I walk into his room. "David?"

No answer. He is lying on his bottom bunk bed, poking the top mattress with his toes.

"David, I want to talk with you." He ignores me, intent on his toe-poking. He is fighting back tears.

I pull up his little red chair beside the bed and sit down. "I feel bad about the way I responded to you, but I just don't know what to do. I don't see how I can just stand by and let you put Kim-

109

berly down like that. It makes her feel so foolish—it seems so unnecessary. Why do you do it?"

No response. He digs his foot deeper into the mattress.

"Do you know why I sent you to your room?"

"I don't want to talk about it."

"I know, but it is too important *not* to talk about. Do you have any idea how much Kimberly looks up to you? You're her big brother, David. What you say is important to her. Can you see how your put-downs make her feel? Foolish and silly in front of someone she desperately wants to impress. Can you see that, David? Can you see why I can't let you treat her that way? You know this home should be a place where we are safe with each other. It is part of my job to see that our home is a safe place. That's why I protected Kimberly from you."

David still is silent, but I feel I'm beginning to make some sense to him.

"There is something else I want you to know. It's not easy being the oldest, always having two little people that want to be around you, always getting into your things and in your way. I know that, I really do. It is also part of my job to protect *you* from them. I know there are times when you need to read or do your homework, or just be alone, and I'll see to it that they leave you alone. If you ask me, I'll see to it that you can be in your room without interruption. How do you feel about that?"

David sits up in his bed and faces me. He looks at me knowingly. "That's right. They *do* get in my way. I'll just let you know when I want to be alone."

"David, will you make a deal with me? If I work to make this home a safe place for you, will you work to make this a safe place for others? Will you?"

He grins sheepishly at me and nods his head.

"Will you go and tell Kimberly you are sorry?"

"Yes."

"Let's shake hands." A bit too enthusiastically he shakes my hand and bounds out of the room, honor restored.

Nothing revolutionary took place, but something was gained. At first I was groping to reach through his resistance to his heart. It seems that our point of contact was my recognition of *his* position; that my understanding of *his* needs became the link to his understanding of Kimberly's needs. He understands the issue and will make an effort toward the right behavior.

This I know—I feel much better about the entire situation. Perhaps nothing of great significance took place, but we took one small step in the right direction—toward maturity. Not just David. Both of us.

LIMITS

The house is "picked up." The breakfast dishes washed. I will reward myself with a free hour and finish the book I'm reading and write a couple of letters.

"Come on, Jonathan. Let's go outside."

"Yeah! Let's go!"

I get Jonathan set up with a tricycle, a bucket, and a shovel. Surrounding myself with pillows, I establish a nice, easy rhythm on the porch swing, and settle in for this happy indulgence. The squeak of the swing is music to my ears. Jonathan chatters to himself, to the squirrels. Shouts to a dog across the street. Cars speed by. Busy people hurry here and there. But *I* am a woman of leisure. Through Henry James's world of complex characters and manners, I am transported to nineteenth-century America.

Silence. Where's Jonathan?

I jump up and rush to the top porch step. Jonathan has walked to the end of the sidewalk and is standing with his toes touching THE LINE—the crack in the sidewalk that has been officially designated as THE LIMIT. Now he squats down, apparently engrossed in a study of an acorn. He pushes it over the line and then walks on his knees to pick it up. Slowly he turns his head to look at me out of the corner of his eye.

I quickly turn. If he doesn't see me see him, I may be able to avoid an inconvenient confrontation. He stands up, rounds the corner, and continues walking toward the back yard. This is past ignoring.

"Come back, honey," I plead. "You *must* play in the front yard."

Jonathan turns to look at me face on, squares his little shoulders, and with full authority says, "*No!*"

"I'll have to spank you if you don't come back right now."

"No."

"Do you want me to carry you back?"

"No."

"OK. You can come back by yourself then."

"No."

"Go get your bike, Jonathan. See how fast you can ride!"

"No."

My heart sinks. The deepest level of my fear has been realized —we've reached an impasse. Jonathan has stepped outside his territory clearly defined by two designated cracks on the sidewalk. I justify my position to myself: The limits confine him to a generous area, fully observable from my snug perch on the front porch. Certain of a comfortable safety margin between the sidewalk and the busy street, I can go about my business with peace of mind.

Daily, Jonathan challenges the limits. Daily, I win, not by persuasion but by brute force—I'm bigger than he. I'm tempted to make one exception, let him go just this time. But I have no choice but to tackle this head on. If I do not get up now I must count for nought the scores (no, hundreds) of times I have previously stopped everything to enforce these limits. Give in now, and the lesson he will learn is this: "*Sometimes* I can go over the line. It is well worth trying it again. I have nothing to lose—and who knows, I may have a great deal to gain!" At the very center of the issue is this unalterable fact: *If I am inconsistent in my discipline this one time, my previous efforts will be to no avail!*

I brace myself for the CONFRONTATION. I stand up, lay down my book, and start walking toward him. Jonathan giggles and runs toward the back yard. I gain on him. He stops laughing as I swoop down and catch him in my arms. I set him down, safely within the limits. He drops to the ground and pounds the concrete with his fists, then lies in a quiet little huddle at my feet. No resistance. His fight is gone. He dissolves into tears of disappointment.

I comfort myself with the sage words of T. Berry Brazilton: Children "learn limits from the outside, then internalize them, which is why discipline is so important. It's a learning process for

113

the child."[4] Is that really true, T. Berry? Can you promise me that? I begin fantasizing the day Jonathan will walk to the line and without so much as a sneak peek over his shoulder, turn around and play within the boundaries determined for him. With joy. "Ah, the freedom of limits," he will declare. And he will rise up and call me blessed!

No, don't answer me. For the time being I'll content myself with this compliant heap before me—and my fantasies. I must go to the porch now and finish reading my chapter.

LEARNING THROUGH FAILURE

David sits at the dining room table, bending over an envelope he is laboriously addressing. This is a Long-Awaited Moment for David. It was love at first sight when he spotted the flashy advertisement for a set of monster cups on the back of the cereal box. After repeatedly refusing to buy them for him, I suggested if it was all that important to him he might want to save up the dollar and send for them himself.

The idea clicked. He began setting aside coins until one day he proudly exchanged a handful of change for a crisp dollar bill. He placed his dollar under the candleholder and began waiting for the cereal box to be emptied. Much like a mother hen watches over her chicks, he watched over the Cheerio box, pushing Cheerios each morning, measuring the level of Cheerios against the height of the box. His scissors were poised as the last round of cereal dropped into a bowl. In a flash the coupon was cut off the box and deftly filled out.

Now he sits on the edge of his chair—tilted so far forward that the back legs lift from the floor—copying the address onto the envelope. Kimberly and Jonathan stand admiringly, each at an elbow. This is an Event.

"Oh no!" David jumps up with a pained expression on his face. "It's ruined!" He thrusts the envelope into my hands. A large smudge from the felt-tip pen scars his carefully formed letters.

"That's OK, David, I have another envelope."

He fights back his tears and begins again. A few minutes later he proudly presents to me his finished product.

"Oh, David, we've got a problem—you did a beautiful job but you wrote on the back of the envelope."

"What am I going to do?"

"It won't take you long to do it again." I hand him another envelope before he can protest.

He sits down and resolutely swings out the address—third go-round. His audience has long disappeared. It is a lonely little figure forlornly working away.

"Mommeeeee!" David shrieks. "I don't have enough room for the return address!" He throws the envelope on the table and stomps out of the room, tears rolling down his face.

My heart sinks. Although I've never shared his enthusiasm for the monster cups, they are beginning to represent the gold-filled pot at the end of the rainbow. Gently I call to David, "I don't blame you a bit if you forget the whole thing, honey—but I've put an envelope on the table just in case you decide to try one more time."

A few minutes later a grimly determined David appears and starts all over again. Finally, wreathed in smiles, he flourishes a flawlessly addressed envelope before my eyes. He places the coupon and dollar bill in the envelope, seals it, and pounds it shut with his fist.

"Great! Now don't mail it until we find a stamp." I head off to get my purse. "Wait right here, I'll be back in a minute."

When I return David is nowhere to be found.

"Where did David go, Kimberly?"

"He went to the mailbox to mail his letter."

"No!" I race out the door and down the stairs only to be greeted by a jubilant David, mission accomplished! "Well, I mailed it. When do you think I'll be getting my cups?"

My heart drops to my feet. "Oh, David," I groan. "Did you put a stamp on it first?"

A look of incredulity sweeps over David's face. "Mommee!" He looks at me with a tell-me-it-isn't-so expression.

"Honey . . . ," I start, taking a step toward him, but before I can continue he has run into the house, most likely to his bottom bunk bed—his place of refuge.

I hear heaving sobs, and then no sound at all. Fighting back my own tears I drop into the big red chair, *my* place of refuge, and mentally review the whole situation: the time involved saving the money and waiting for the cereal box to empty, his "addressing" efforts—clearly a task beyond his experience—the wasted dollar. Everything within me shouts, buy another box of cereal, advance him a dollar, fill out an envelope. Make things right for him.

But another voice speaks, barely audible above my feelings, but clearly nonetheless and logically. What was his fatal flaw in this fiasco? Not listening. "Don't mail it until we find a stamp . . . Wait right here," I had said, but he hadn't heard because he wasn't listening—like a hundred times before. "But I didn't hear you" he always counters and little is learned because little has been lost for him. Now he has made a mistake that has cost him dearly. Will I intervene or will I let him learn from his failure. I think of what Paul Tournier says about the part failure plays in our growth:

> It is through a series of experiences of failure that the child gradually discovers the world and its proper relationship with himself. Every baby stretches out his hands to the lamp on the ceiling and cries because he cannot reach it. By falling he learns to walk. Through many misunderstandings he learns to express himself better. Through awkwardness and mala-droitness he learns new movements and new activities, and through understanding why he fails he learns new skills. After the sweeping enthusiasms of adolescence he will experience many failures, which will teach him to apportion his ambition to his ability, so as to realize something concrete instead of keeping everything in the realm of dreams.
>
> Throughout his life his laborious progress along a failure-strewn road will be his training for manhood . . . Someday he will understand that our successes benefit others, but our failures benefit ourselves.[5]

I will leave him alone for a while to sort out his feelings. Then I'll go to him with my love and sympathy and see if we can talk about what happened. Perhaps together we can turn his mistake into a growth-producing experience.

RESPONSIBILITY

What a mess! I look around Kimberly's toy-strewn room. What on earth is David's sock doing in here? I walk into David's room to return his sock and am greeted by a room that appears to be competing with Kimberly's for the Mess of the Year Award. This is the limit! I've already gone throughout the house picking up misplaced items. Crayons and coloring books. Pajamas, in a heap on the bathroom floor. A pile of books on the television. Sweaters and jackets on the floor *beneath* their wall hooks.

The children know only too well they are responsible for keeping their rooms clean and returning personal possessions to their rightful places. It is not as if I don't remind them. "David, have you put your books away?" "Kimberly, don't forget to hang up your coat." When David shouts, "I can't find my spelling words," I point out, "If you had put them on the high chair, like you were *supposed* to, you'd have no problem finding them now, would you?" "Well, Kimberly, you know where your coat is *supposed* to be, don't you! Maybe this will be a lesson for the next time." But it isn't. I grow old picking up items that should have been put away. The children atrophy as I carry out *their* responsibilities.

I begin to think of their extra jobs. They have been clearly designated and reinforced by pictures pasted to magnets on the refrigerator door. (Pictures, I might add, that have been ingeniously designed by their clever mother.) When was the last time they carried out those jobs—*without being told?* I begin to smolder. Apart from the burden it places on me, what does this represent in terms of their ability to shoulder a little responsibility? I have tried to be reasonable in what I expect of them. I have taken into consideration individual preferences and have designated jobs that are not contrived but are really needed for a well-functioning

118

household. We have tried to communicate the importance of their contribution and have affirmed them for good work. What has gone wrong? Are they in reality what they appear to me this moment to be—perverse and lazy little parasites? Or is it possible, in some small, remote sort of way, *I* have fallen short?

I have to admit I've been inconsistent in enforcing the rules. Sometimes I insist they carry out their jobs, sometimes I don't. Often it's easier to do it myself than to motivate them. Or circumstances throw us out of our routines and we just don't get back into the swing again. So I say one thing, but they hear another thing because my inconsistency in following up my words in effect shouts this louder message—it really isn't that important.

When seen as simply a misplaced sock or a messy room, it *doesn't* seem all that important. After all, children will be children. But when seen in terms of learning to take responsibility and all that involves—work habits, self-discipline, co-operation, obedience, consideration for others—it becomes an entirely different issue. And a very important one. Their daily approach to responsibility now, however insignificant it may seem, becomes a pattern they will carry with them into other aspects of their lives for the rest of their lives. As a parent, I have a responsibility to do the best I can to equip them for life. Isn't our approach to our work, whatever that may be, and our response to authority, whoever that may be, a very significant part of our adult life? I look around the cluttered room. I remove the mental label I have given it—PERSONAL ANNOYANCE—and replace it with a different one—GROWTH OPPORTUNITY.

When the children come home we've got some talking to do. While I will try to communicate to them the bigger issue, I can assume they will continue to resist the work and challenge the rules until they become a consistently enforced part of their routine. Together we must come up with ways of making *them* bear the consequences of their inaction rather than resorting to my ineffective "nagging and prodding" method.

It won't be easy. It would be much easier to do the work myself. But I must daily remind myself that the real issue is not a clean room, an empty trash can, or toys in their proper places. The real issue—and one worthy of sacrifice on my part—is the shaping of character.

WHO'S INFLUENCING MY CHILDREN?

"Can we watch TV, Mom?" David sets his books and lunch box on the high chair and looks at me with bright hope and expectancy. It never fails to amaze me how he faithfully asks this question that through the years has been consistently answered in the negative.

"Not until four o'clock, honey."

"How come?"

"You know we never watch TV right after school. This is your time to play." I answer with what strikes me, under the circumstances, as a monumental show of patience.

"*Everyone* watches TV after school."

"That's right," echoes Kimberly. "*Everyone*."

"I doubt that," I respond, measuring each word carefully. "But even if they did, you know that isn't how we make our decisions."

"I'll choose a good program that won't scare Kimberly and Jonathan."

"The programs aren't bad, Mommy," Kimberly adds.

"I know the programs aren't bad, but I just don't think anything is on now that is *that* good." I go on to explain how precious time is, how many good things there are to do. We limit TV because we want them to *live* life, not just sit back and watch *others* live life.

David and Kimberly look up at me with expressions that simulate total incomprehension. David shrugs his shoulders and says, "C'mon, Kimberly, let's go ride our bikes."

Am I too strict? I ask myself. There is nothing in the programs they are pushing for that is harmful. After a busy day in school, shouldn't they just be free to sit back and be entertained for a while? I review our policy: They have a daily block of time set aside for their choice of several pre-determined programs. We check the TV guide for specials which we attempt to make a shared family time. Then there are their morning fragments of "Captain Kangaroo." No, in proportion to their other activities, they see plenty of television!

I begin to bristle that I let myself be put into a defensive position. I'm convinced we approach the whole thing from the wrong angle—if it's not bad, it's OK we allow, rather than *choosing* from the enormous smorgasbord of programs that which is edifying and good. By default, we've let the question become "Why not?" rather than "Why?" making it a matter of acquiescence rather than choice.

I mount my soapbox and continue to build a defense of our position. I think of the vast number of messages our children are subjected to, input that is shaping their thinking and in turn their character. I am realistic; I can't put blinders on my children, and even if I could, I wouldn't. TV is only one of the many voices that shout their conflicting messages, that have something to say about everything. But it happens to be one influence I can still control. There is so much at stake. When you cut through it all—the mundane activities surrounding mothering—my deepest concern is the kind of people our children are becoming. They cannot help but be influenced by the values that bombard them. Values so often in conflict with what we are trying to stress; the importance of the inner man, the person we really are—in a word, character.

I don't want to tune out other messages altogether. I just want to keep up with their input so I can help them learn to be discerning. I will not always be able to screen their TV input, but I refuse to abdicate my filtering role while my children are still so moldable simply because of their demands, or because it is expedient for me.

By now I am gesturing eloquently from my soapbox and am becoming increasingly possessed with a desire to dismount and rip the TV from its life line on the wall. Show it a thing or two. But I begin to cool as I consider how it has enriched our lives: the concerts we've enjoyed in the comfort of our sitting room, our trips to faraway lands, the exposure to values and life-styles of another time and place, drama that has carried our emotions the full gamut—together . . . When I hear Jonathan count to thirteen, I have to admit he didn't learn his numbers from me! So I kick my soapbox aside, and reassume a more realistic posture, that of a mother simply trying to make decisions that will be in the best interest of her family.

No, like most everything else, the TV is not inherently good or evil. It holds the potential for either. The fundamental issue is, who is in control? The TV? Or are we in control? I believe it places far too great a burden on the grade school child to have to make these quality-of-life decisions. As parents, we will continue to assume the responsibility of determining the amount of time spent watching TV and the kind of programs watched. We will continue to allow our children choices within our choices, knowing the day will come when they must exercise their own judgment. I would hope by then we will have established a pattern of selection that will provide a kind of inner monitoring for their own positive choices.

ON THE NEED FOR WISDOM

A lamp has been broken, pulled off the wall. The owner graciously insists it is not valuable; it can easily be replaced. How did it happen? No adult was in the room at the time; only Jonathan and Kimberly were there. Kimberly claims it was not her fault—Jonathan did it. However, the evidence is overwhelmingly against her. The only possible way a child could pull it from the wall would be to put his whole weight on it. It is above Jonathan's reach; Kimberly is a born climber and swinger. It is all too easy for me to picture what happened.

Now at home I try to deal with the situation.

"What really happened to the lamp, Kimberly?"

"Jonathan broke it."

"You didn't actually see him do it, though, did you?"

"No, but he did it."

I sit down on the floor next to Kimberly, who is fiddling with her shoelaces. "Kimberly, let me tell you what I think happened. Jonathan is too little to reach the lamp, so he couldn't have done it. I think you were playing and without even thinking, grabbed onto the lamp. Before you knew it, the lamp came loose. You probably felt so bad you just couldn't admit it."

"I didn't do it."

"Kimberly, it really isn't important whether you did it or not. Not nearly as important as telling the truth. No one is going to punish you—the lamp can be replaced. But honey, I'll feel so much better, and you'll feel so much better, if you just admit you did it."

Kimberly raises a perfectly guileless face and looks straight into my eyes. "But I didn't do it, Mommy. *Really*, I didn't."

What do I do now? I wasn't there. Is it possible she didn't do it? I've been assured Jonathan *couldn't* have done it. But could his agility have been underestimated? No. We'd discussed it thoroughly and determined it simply wasn't possible. I can see what has happened. A pleaser by nature, Kimberly works hard to do the right thing. It would be difficult for her to accept she'd broken something in the first place. Now the issue is complicated by her lie—she's worked herself into a corner and she is unable to come out.

I start in again, explaining it is all right about the lamp; it is not all right about the lie. I understand how hard it is to back down but won't she "just tell what really happened so we can clear up the whole thing and forget it?" Around and around we go, Kimberly insisting the whole time on her innocence.

Finally, under pressure, she says, "I don't know who did it, but *if* I did it, I don't *remember* doing it."

Now what do I say? The issue is on new ground—"*Maybe* I did it, but I don't remember doing it." Not my idea of a confession! Do I now pursue whether she remembers it or not? Do I punish her for lying? Make her apologize for something she claims she can't remember doing? Drop the issue entirely? We've reached a dead end and I simply don't know what to do.

". . . if any of you lacks wisdom, he should pray to God, who will give it to him; because God gives generously and graciously to all."[6]

Dear Father in Heaven, I have to act now but I am at a loss as to what to do. Give me the wisdom to deal rightly with this situation.

If I have already erred in my judgment, protect this child, for you are her Heavenly Father. May the consequences of my action not be too severe for her to sustain.

Release me from the fear that accompanies the uncertainty of my decision. I, too, am your child, Father. I need you.

Once I have dealt with this matter to the best of my ability, help me to rest it in Your hands—recognizing and acknowledging my limitations—and be at peace. Amen.

CHRISTIAN EDUCATION—WHOSE JOB?

And thou shalt love the Lord thy God with all thine heart, and with all thy soul, and with all thy might.

And these words, which I command thee this day, shall be in thine heart:

And thou shalt teach them diligently unto thy children, and shalt talk of them when thou sittest in thine house, and when thou walkest by the way, and when thou liest down, and when thou risest up.

And thou shalt bind them for a sign upon thine hand, and they shall be as frontlets between thine eyes.

And thou shalt write them upon the posts of thy house, and on thy gates.[7]

Does this Old Testament plan for the spiritual nurture of children apply today? I believe so. In fact, I'm struck with its relevancy for my generation of parents. We have turned so much of the training of our children over to highly qualified organizations. Whose responsibility *is* the Christian education of our children? Where can it be done most effectively? Certainly the church plays an important role. But this passage seems to present the *ideal*—parents training the children in the home. In essence it says: The teaching of Scripture should be thoroughly integrated into all aspects of daily living by parents committed to God and grounded in Scripture.

This makes sense. The most effective learning *is* that which arises from real-life experiences. I see the challenge here of taking from everyday living opportunities to apply biblical concepts. Then teaching is relevant rather than isolated from children's experience. If Christian education is to be totally integrated into daily living, it becomes obvious that the church can only be a supportive or, if necessary, substitute education.

Take biblical standards. Thou shalt not lie. Words. But they take on an entirely different meaning when a child has become entangled in a complicated web of lies. How do I feel when I tell a lie? How does one lie grow into more lies? How does it affect other people? What is the best way to resolve the situation? Children begin to understand the "why" behind God's laws, as they look at the real consequences of their behavior.

Every good teacher looks for the right questions that will create curiosity on the part of the learner to set the stage for effective teaching. As parents we can take the questions that come up naturally from everyday situations and turn them into vital teaching experiences. We can relate them to biblical concepts and hopefully back them up with our own current experiences.

Virtues . . . Honesty. Perseverance. Responsibility. Kindness. Faithfulness. Loyalty. We can discuss them in isolation. But that learning can't be compared to what takes place when we walk together through situations where these qualities are demonstrated, *then* talked about. Children *understand* loyalty when we stand by each other through a rough time. We can follow this up by pointing out Bible characters who exemplify this quality—Jonathan. Or people who don't—Joseph's brothers.

Whether I intend to or not, I *am* teaching my children each day. The issue is *what* am I teaching them? "And these words, which I command thee this day, shall be in thine heart. And thou shalt teach them diligently unto thy children . . ."[8]

Dear God, make me sensitive to the opportunities to teach my children about You that arise in the course of everyday living. How easily I become caught up with daily pressures and details and lose the more important over-all perspective of the bigger scheme. Unintentionally I squeeze the Christian nurture of our children into small specified blocks of time, or delegate the teaching to the church. Unthinkingly, a clean floor can take precedence over answering a child's question. Keeping on schedule crowds out a potential learning situation.

O Lord, make me ever conscious of the subtle enemy that turns everything upside down for me—reversed priorities. May I make a habit of putting first the things you consider important.

May I be responsible to the precious trust you put into my keeping—my children. Give me divine wisdom as I seek to answer their questions and deal with each daily challenge. May my life lend credibility to my words, that I will not stand in the way of their developing a vital relationship with you. Amen.

MODELING

Kimberly is scheduled for a preschool physical examination this morning. Recalling my own childhood apprehensions, I prepare her for what she will encounter. Taking measurements. Undressing. I mention the possibility of shots.

We arrive at the doctor's office with Kimberly in high spirits. She runs off to play with the toys. Her name is called. She cooperates fully with the weigh-in and stands up tall for her measurements. Blithely she crosses the hall to the examining room.

The nurse smiles at Kimberly and says, "You can take off your shoes, stockings, shirt, and slacks, dear. The doctor will be right in."

Kimberly looks stricken. "Mommy, what if someone *sees* me?"

"The door is closed tightly."

"Will you lock it?"

"Then the doctor can't come in."

"I can't let the doctor see me without my *clothes* on!" Her little face looks white and drawn.

"That's OK, honey. That's just a part of his job. He does it all day long. All the children in your classroom had to undress for their examination."

She doesn't make a single movement. Her eyes are brimming with tears. Her lips are trembling. "Mommy, if you were me, would *you* do it?"

I sense how much is at stake for her. "Yes, Kimberly," I say positively, "I certainly would."

Without another word Kimberly removes each specified article of clothing and climbs up on the examination table.

"If you were me, would *you* do it?" How many times has an

affirmative answer to that question settled Kimberly's indecision once and for all. "If Mommy would do it, it must be all right." Modeling—conscious and open.

I think of Dave and little David golfing on a par three course. David matching stride with his father, even assuming that subtle suggestion of a swagger, "C'mon, Mom, join us." I catch the look of conspiracy that passes between father and son. A kind of "bear with her" look, "she's only a beginner." So I join them to be constantly reassured by David—"Good one!" "Aw, you'll do better next time." "Did you see her swing, Dad?" "Hey, Mom's really good." Where have I heard those phrases before? David continually eggs me on, encouraging where he can, ignoring the hard to ignore, unconsciously but exactingly modeling his father.

Jonathan—almost a caricature of modeling—spends a good part of his waking hours studying his older counterparts, checking out their every movement, then executing his faithful imitations. I can picture him sitting at the breakfast table, eyes tightly shut in prayer, with an almost beatific expression on his face (much like St. Francis of old, I'm sure), mouthing syllables, meaningfully (if mindlessly), winding up with an emphatic "A-men!"

Modeling. Like breathing, they model. Day in and day out they observe and pick up cues about how to act or react in particular situations. How much of what they are observing and patterning from us is in conflict with what we believe and teach? How many times have we negatively affected their attitudes by subtle innuendoes or unconscious intonation?

We can preach, teach, moralize, exhort, and discipline, but nothing, no nothing, influences them so consistently or convincingly as our lives. Is my life one I want my children to model?

5

The Family—
A Greenhouse for
Relationships

"You taught us to take seriously our relationship as a family. We were required to treat each family member with at least the same interest and respect as we would our friends. After all, 'How can we expect to get along with others if we don't first learn to live with those closest to us?'"

FULL-BARREL LEARNING

"Don't unwind the ladder."

"Kimberly, it's *my* fire engine."

"I know, but I was playing with it."

"When I walked in the room you were playing with the *castle*."

"But I was coming right back to the engine, David. You know I was."

"You only want the fire engine because I have it."

"That's not true. I was playing with it. Don't unwind the ladder!"

"Kimberly! Get away! IT'S MY FIRE ENGINE!"

"DAVID! STOP IT!!!"

I listen. I wait. It's possible they can sort this one out for themselves. If they can't, they'll come to me, fervently setting forth their separate cases. There is no doubt about it, it is irritating to hear them go at it. I have to restrain myself from going in and barking exactly how I feel about the situation. But I know something much more important than the issue of the moment is taking place. They are learning full-barrel what people do and do not like; what is acceptable and unacceptable behavior from another person's point of view. Lessons that will serve them well in life.

I think of a statement made by Catherine Marshall after eight years of raising a second family. "I see more clearly than ever what the Creator must have had in mind by decreeing that we be born as babies into families rather than, say, springing full-grown out of bushes. Surely, it must be because the family is meant to be the training ground for life, a true microcosm of the world outside the home."[1] What better place could there be to learn to get along with other people than surrounded by one's own most loving assortment of people?

Through this intense daily contact not only do we find the opportunity to develop skills in relating to others, but something positive can happen to our own self as well. Elisabeth Elliot says, "And it is in relation to other people that we ourselves become full persons."[2] Our selfish persons are shaped and refined as we come up against the wills and needs of other people in a situation we cannot easily walk out on.

It's not easy to live in harmony with other people. But when I consider that I value the people I love more than anything else on earth, nothing seems to be too great an investment toward that end. I'm determined to do my part in guiding our children toward this understanding. As we face conflicts through day-to-day living, I would hope that my actions will back up my words, that together we will grow in understanding and that we will assist each other in becoming the people we could be.

FATHER MAGIC

"Mommy, I just *love* Daddy!" declares Kimberly.

"I know."

"I love you, too, but Daddy is a lot specialer than you!"

I'm tempted to remind her of all the wonderful things *I* do day in and day out for her unappreciative little self, but concede instead that Daddy *is* "a lot specialer." Would I, who too have known the incomparable security and excitement that a father imparts to his young, begrudge him that title so lovingly bestowed on him? I consider for a moment what it is that makes a father "specialer"—for indeed he is!

At the core of it all must be the overwhelming sense of strength his very presence imparts. "My daddy is the strongest man in the world." What does this universal child claim really mean? That to a child's heart there is no safer place than within the circle of his father's love. Strength. Security. Refuge. Little matter if to the world he be sot or king—for whatever the child feels him to be, *that* he is.

As if that is not enough, he holds the wonderful, enchanted element of serendipity. I'm not such a romantic as to claim that all is made right by the proclamation "Daddy's home!" but never are the children more inclined to forget grudges, set aside issues, shed irritability, than when Daddy appears into their little world like a shock of joy. Oh, to possess such magic!

Is it fair that one individual should hold such power? (Especially one who can account for so few hours of the children's day?) While at times I do believe I'd sell my soul for one chance at the "wand," I know that Dave is not the only one to profit from their bewitchment. All that he contributes feeds into the total investment being made for these children—*our* children. We each have designated areas of responsibilities in which we invest for efficient home management, but the children are *our* investment. What kind of fool would seriously resent a deposit in a joint account?

Furthermore, whatever he contributes to them indirectly contributes to me—lightens my load. Truthfully, if Dave is home, rare is the night I would be permitted to preside over the detailed bedtime ceremonies. Poor Dave! What a lift those moments (and others) give me!

I not only accept Dave's special place in the children's hearts, but I rejoice in it. And I believe that if none of these benefits passed my way I still would not begrudge him his father magic, for though the spell days are numbered, at best, there is no human alive who, having experienced them, does not carry a bit of the magic in his heart to his dying day.

PARENT OR FRIEND?

"You're not my friend any more!" A thwarted David stalks haughtily from my presence. His rejection stabs right through me. I want to grab my child and say, "Like me—be my friend. Can't you see I'm only doing what's best for you?" But this is not the time for reason. His will has been crossed; his words accurately express his sentiments.

A friend or a parent—what am I? I'd *like* to be both, but sometimes the two just don't mix. To be a friend is to love and accept a person just as he is. But I'm told a child needs *more* than love and acceptance:

> Although love is essential to human life, parental responsibility extends far beyond it . . . Love in the absence of instruction will not produce a child with self-discipline, self-control, and respect for his fellow man. Affection and warmth underlie all mental and physical health, yet they do not eliminate the need for careful training and guidance . . .
>
> Respectful and responsible children result from families where the proper combination of *love* and *discipline* is present.[3]

To be a parent involves instruction and discipline, elements which, from a child's point of view, are irreconcilable with friendship. Friend or parent? To be one, at times, precludes the other.

Do I really have a choice? Is it not God's design that I be first a parent? Looking at it this way helps me: Children *need* parents. Other people will be friends to my children, but no one else will be their parent. Would I deprive my children because of *my* desire to be considered a friend?

In the total picture, the times of being "out of grace" are relatively few and brief. Children are not grudge bearers. How quickly their love eclipses the bad times—"I love you this (arms outstretched, fingers touching behind the back) much." What mother heart has not been sent soaring by a child's declaration, "You are the most beautiful lady in the whole wide world"? And the challenge—to have a significant hand in someone's destiny—is reason enough to have lived! Is it so bad to be a *parent?*

I must remind myself that relationships are not static. The day will come when I must set free my adult child by relinquishing the parent role. This, then, will be my compensation: the potential for a new kind of relationship—a friendship. If I do my job correctly now, it is more likely my children will be the kind of people I will value as lifelong friends.

NOBODY'S PERFECT!

"Ow!" I strike my ankle on a sharp projection. What is the lawn mower doing in the middle of the garage! I grope my way through semidarkness to my destination. As I work to dislodge the desired box another box falls on my shoulder and crashes to the floor. When is Dave ever going to clean *his* garage!

Once in the house I make a point of walking through the sitting room, where Dave is absorbed in a football game.

"The garage is a mess."

"Uh huh."

"You said you were going to clean it."

"I am."

"When?"

"I don't know, for sure."

How can Dave just sit there and watch TV with the garage in such a condition? He knows good and well if he doesn't clean it now it will be another week before he could even consider doing it. And would he be any more inclined to do it then than he is today, or was last week, or the week before . . . ? As I go about my Saturday chores, working this over in my mind, a clean garage becomes a matter of increasing importance. Images of all the clean and perfectly ordered garages I've seen recently march in a spotless review before me. I work more vigorously, making no effort to keep down my work noises. I become suddenly aware of my smarting ankle. An errand compels me to pass in front of Dave. I punish him with silence. It is unheeded and, I suspect, completely unnoticed. Now my ankle hurts in earnest!

Kindled by the fire of my mounting case against Dave, I continue my zealous cleaning. But a thought hostile to my present state of mind elbows its way to my consciousness. I try to resist this intruder but now other images persistently wedge their way in. I vaguely can see a hamper overflowing with dirty clothes. Then a stack of unironed shirts behind the armoire. And what's that next to them? Clothing that needs mending! I can only hope Dave's mind is so full of football that there is no room for such thoughts!

Why is it that I continue to insist on perfection from Dave when I know only too well how far short *I* fall below the mark?

> When people insist on perfection or nothing, they get nothing . . . The waste of what could be, by demanding what cannot be, is something we all have lived through in certain periods of our lives, but which we need to put behind us with resolve.[4]

Here I am, wasting a potentially pleasant Saturday afternoon by concentrating on Dave's failure to meet my expectations. I can choose to focus on Dave's imperfections, or accept them as a small part of the person I love.

As much as I wish he gloried in the cleaning and ordering of garages, it is unlikely he will ever become a great lover of such things. I might clean the garage myself or, at a more opportune time, offer to help him. (Perhaps it won't be cleaned at all!) But for now I will accept things as they are and absolve Dave from his "sin" of neglect.

With a heart years lighter I go in and bestow a kiss of forgiveness on a blissfully unaware Dave!

A BRAND-NEW START

Sunday morning. Once again I ponder my weekly question: "Would I rather be Dave refining the morning sermon, or me preparing three children for church?" David and Kimberly have been at each other since they woke up. At the breakfast table it only takes a glance from one or a motion toward their "territory" to set off the other. To even thank Jesus for the food seems out of place with the spirit of the moment.

In a last-ditch attempt to redeem the morning, I suggest we "ask Jesus to forgive us and give us a brand-new start." With relief they agree and I can almost feel the air clear with the final "Amen."

Tonight I rush about trying to put the house in order for a meeting. Time is short, the work overwhelming, and the children "too much with me." But single-mindedly I keep working toward my goal. David, who has been around the edges of things, stills me with a question.

"Mommy? Do you want to stop right now and ask Jesus for a brand-new start?"

There is no mistaking the implication of his suggestion. I begin to launch into my self-defense when I'm caught up short by David's look of total sincerity.

Yes, it's true that I'm under pressure with a time factor that can't absorb interruption. But from his point of view I'm abrupt, short-off, and badly in need of a "brand-new start!"

I resist the urge to wield my parental authority by dismissing his comment as "out of line." I may be the parent but when it comes to a spiritual pilgrimage we are brothers and sisters in

Christ. Am I willing to accept his perception of my behavior and learn from him?

I stop my work to apologize to David for my impatience. Together, we take a moment to ask Jesus "for a new start for Mommy." Silently I continue my prayer, asking God to help me live a life that will not contradict my words.

RENDEZVOUS

"I have friends that are girls, but I don't really have a girl friend," David confides.

"What is the difference betwen a girl that is a friend and a girl friend?"

"Well, you have to kiss girl friends, and maybe even marry them someday."

The occasion of this intimate exchange was David's Monday night tea party—his time to stay up after everyone else had been tucked in. He carefully arranged the antique tea set (reserved solely for this purpose) on the breakfast room table, poured apple juice into the teapot, and placed oatmeal cookies on tiny tea plates. At his request I lit the candles and turned off the light. The stage was set . . .

If I ever questioned for a moment the value of setting aside this extra time—one night a week for David, another night for Kimberly—all doubt was erased the evening David abruptly interrupted our festivities. He jumped from his seat, ran over to me, and standing a mere nose length away looked deep into my eyes. "Do you know what I'm thinking? I LOVE YOU!!!" He sealed his statement by planting an emphatic kiss smack on my mouth. That night the tea party became a tradition!

Our weekly rendezvous guarantees us quality time together. It seems like I'm always with the children, but I can easily fail to spend time alone with each child. During this time I make a special effort to draw them out, encouraging them to share the high points and low points of the week. Unhurried, without fear of interruption, hearts are opened, dreams and fears risked, secrets shared.

142

To say each evening is filled with deep conversation and insightful exchanges would not be entirely accurate. There was the night David told "knock knock" jokes for one hour straight, making up his own material when his repertoire was exhausted. One evening Kimberly skipped clear around the dining room table each time she completed a sentence. I was sustained through those evenings (and others) by reminding myself of tea parties more overtly profitable!

Between tea parties the fragile gold-rimmed teapot, plates, cups, and saucers wait in proud display on a shelf in the dining room. As David and Kimberly catch sight of the little tea set amid their comings and goings, I would hope they would be reminded in their spirits of its special message—that what they think and say is important. May it serve as a glowing monument to their immeasurable worth.

ON YELLING

Yelling again . . . I'm rushed. I'm tired. The children roughly tumble through the kitchen knocking things down along the way. I'm angry, so I yell. Now they know just how I feel. Sober and sheepish, they evaporate from me.

Modern psychology says it's good to express emotions. "It's healthy," they say. Healthy for me—no repression for me. But is it healthy for these children of mine? Modern psychology answers me: "Yes, better to have it out in the open. Clear the air." Healthy for them. Healthy for me. Why, then, do I feel so bad?

I think of a friend's experience as a graduate student at the University of Michigan. Now carillonneur at Bok Tower at Mountain Lake Sanctuary, he was then preparing for his master's organ recital. He tells of attempting to fit practice time into his hectic teaching schedule. Then, work-weary, he traveled two hundred miles to the university to continue his musical preparation. One week before the recital he performed for his teacher, who sat in the back of the auditorium. When he completed Bach's imposing *Passacaglia and Fugue,* his teacher came up to him and asked him how he felt about his performance. He pushed him further by asking how many mistakes he thought he made.

"Oh, a half dozen or so."

At that point the teacher produced a sheet of paper that contained no less than fifty checks, each indicating a time a mistake was made. My friend instantly launched into a recitation of indisputable excuses. His teacher listened patiently, then responded by simply stating, "You know your excuses—I know them too. But next week when you perform before an audience, it won't be your excuses which will be heard. It will be your mistakes!"

144

Something deep inside me responds to his experience. For in spite of all my excuses, I know my performance counts—at least to me. Maybe it is good for me to unleash my negative emotions. Maybe it won't hurt my children. But for each excuse-justified yell there is a black mark for performance. And this is not the way I want to "perform" in my family. I know without a doubt it contradicts the atmosphere I strive to create in our home.

In spite of the experts, I have this lingering question: What effect *could* my reactions have on my vulnerable young? I don't know what goes on in their tender hearts; that which might bounce right off one child, unnoticed, could strike deeply into the heart of another. I'm resilient. I'm adult. Yet I know how I shrink inwardly when I am the object of another's emotional release, even when I understand why. I find I'm not satisfied with the two options before me—repressing or expressing.

I clipped an article some time ago which was promptly lost. It presented a third option: processing the anger. How this was developed, I can't remember; but I like the word: processing. I like the way it fits between the opposite poles of repression and expression: processing . . .

Let me do a retake on my earlier performance, but this time with some "processing." In they stumble, knocking things down along the way. I feel anger. I accept my feelings without guilt. But now, what will I do with my feelings? Shout them out? No. This time I will try to process these feelings in a way that I can live with—that they can live with. I will tell them how their actions make me feel and why, and what I will do if it happens again. And I will do what I say when it does happen again, for it probably will. Anger dealt with through constructive processing— there is something vigorously positive for all of us in that.

Oh, I know I'll fail—and I'll fortify myself with excuses. I'll take comfort from the experts who tell me it's OK. But I'm convinced that there is a better way, and for that I will strive.

> I will try to walk a blameless path, but how I need Your help, especially in my own home where I long to act as I should.[5]

ANNIVERSARY REFLECTIONS

"With all my love, David." I lift the bouquet from its florist box and set it in a silver Victorian cake dish. I step back to admire the sweetheart roses, white and pink, set amid dainty sprigs of babies'-breath. It's lovely—it's perfect! It is also my single consolation for being inappropriately apart from Dave on this our twelfth anniversary.

As I gaze at the bouquet, time fades and I find myself looking at a bridal bouquet secured to a mother-of-pearl Bible. Our wedding day. Images float freely . . . a whirl of friends and relatives arriving for the festivities bearing gifts and "catch-up" chatter; bridesmaids in pretty dresses, flowers; the stillness of the candle-lit church broken only by organ music; the groom smiling reassuringly at the end of that never-ending aisle. But above all other impressions, as clear and distinct as if it were today, is my bride heart . . . filled with young love and high ideals.

It didn't take long to discover that marriage demanded far more than shining hopes and great expectations. Elisabeth Elliot says, "love does not preserve marriage—marriage preserves love."[6] I believe she is right. How many times in that past twelve years has our commitment to marriage forced us to settle down and work things out when it would have been infinitely easier to walk away. As I reflect on our relationship, two things stand out as the positive active ingredients: communication with the goal of understanding each other; and the willingness to adapt—to accept workable solutions instead of demanding the non-existent perfect solution. Ingredients which always contribute to a positive resolve and a deeper relationship.

Communication. How can two people learn to understand each

other if they don't express their thoughts and feelings? Learning to communicate effectively requires different things of each of us. For Dave it means talking when he would far rather "forget it," in the hope that it will "blow over." For me it means guarding myself from overreacting, which discourages Dave from sharing; and learning to drop a subject that has been exhausted.

We've discovered, through trial and error, there is infinitely more to communication than "telling it like it is." If our goal is increased understanding, it will require communicating in a way that does not "put off" the other person or set up defense barriers that stand in the way of being heard. For us, good communication has been implemented by learning to share feelings rather than statements of fact. It is easier to accept "I feel bad when you are out so many evenings" than the subjective judgment "You are never at home." When we communicate our feelings with valid empathy, we are heard more clearly; the more clearly we are heard, the greater is the possibility of increased understanding.

Adaptation is the necessary next step from effective communication. When we come to really understand the other person's point of view the only thing left standing in the way of attempting a workable compromise is selfishness. Declaring my own rights and selfless living are mutually exclusive.

Yielding to Dave's leadership requires me, at points, to give up certain rights, just as Dave, for the nurture of our relationship, relinquishes the exclusive rights to his time, money, and choices.

Much of the "submitting" to each other is done easily and unconsciously out of love, but when our rights collide it requires adaptation—sometimes a painful, though often creative, process. A process which inevitably results in better people, and often a mutually satisfactory solution.

I see again my lovely bouquet—signifying twelve years of marriage. Good years. Happy years. Years that have stretched both of us as we learned to accommodate the needs and wills of the other person.

> "Down on your knees and thank Heaven fasting, for a good man's love."[7]

147

OUT-OF-BOUNDS BOY

Screams, shrieks. Now crying. I run into the sitting room and find three bodies piled in one flailing heap. It doesn't take long to discover David is the culprit. It seems he nosedived from the sofa and crash-landed on Kimberly and Jonathan seated on the floor below. Jonathan covers his head with one hand, clutches his shoulder with the other, wailing above David's desperate protestation of innocence. Kimberly stops crying long enough to isolate the precise spot of contact from her head-on collision with Jonathan.

This action is consistent with the rest of David's day. He has raced from room to room with an imaginary football, catching "passes," stopping only to hike the "ball"; he bounced a balloon from his head, keeping it in perpetual motion, furniture no obstacle. When I suggested he go outside to play he slammed the door behind him, shaking the entire house.

Now he looks at me with puzzled hurt. It is clear to me he meant no harm; his intentions were the finest. Out-of-bounds boy, what do I do with you? Your voice is too loud. Your reactions too quick. You run when you should walk. This home is not big enough to absorb your rough play. You have more energy than hours to expend it. High-spirited, you passionately live out each minute of your day. What do I do with you?

Understand you. Let me above all remember that you are a child—and not demand too much from you. First child, it seems there has always been someone younger than you; more has been expected from you than the other children. But that makes you no more than what you are—a seven-year-old boy. May your buoyancy be a constant reminder to me of this fact, that I might delight in your childishness.

Appreciate you. May I capitalize on those positive qualities that stem from your boundless enthusiasm. You invest such energy in your tasks. When you *do* clean your room, you pull it apart and put it back together with unequaled fervor. If you are supposed to read twenty books, you'll read fifty; fifty books, you'll read one hundred. You laugh the loudest at our sparkling wit, enjoy to the fullest whatever adventure we offer. Point you in the right direction, equip you with the proper materials—watch out, world!

Love you. A child who demands limits, you may not understand discipline to be the back side of love. I must demonstrate my love through my words, by the time I spend with you, through a physical closeness. You may pull away from an insensitive display of affection, but you snuggle closely when we read together; caught up in conversation you take us engagingly by the hand; hug us tightly when you are tucked in. Would that I take my cues from you.

Out-of-bounds boy, what do I do with you? Understand you! Appreciate you! Love you!

DUMPING ON DAVE

Dave is home! This is the bright moment I have been anticipating throughout an exceedingly trying day. The children race to
greet him; I impatiently await my turn. Finally the children dis-
perse and I go in to "dump" on Dave the trials and tribulations of
my day.

He is sprawled comfortably across the couch, his face hidden
behind a newspaper. Without relinquishing his hold on the newspaper he shifts it to one side and makes an admirable effort to appear interested. I talk, trying to ignore his impassive face, his va-
cant eyes. But I cannot ignore his "Oh yes" when his obvious
response should be "No, you don't mean it." There could be no
clearer evidence of what I've been suspecting all along—he is not
really listening.

I stand and leave the room. Dave makes not even the slightest
restraining gesture.

I resume my meal preparation against exasperating odds—
David and Kimberly talking to me in unison, the insistent ringing
of the phone, a smelly Jonathan clinging to my legs, and most of
all my overwhelming exhaustion. As the pressure builds, my frustration mounts. Here I am, trying to co-ordinate the impossible.
There sits Dave in easy comfort, indifferent to my needs. Sure
wish *I* could take a nice little break. The least he could do is
change Jonathan's diaper!

With a stab of guilt I recall a quote from the book *Women and
Sometimes Men:* "One of the most poignant paradoxes in the life
of a woman is that when a man comes to her, he so often comes
to recover his simple humanity and to rest from being at his
best."[8] What has *Dave's* day been like? From what demands and
pressures does *he* need to recover?

And what has happened to my dreams of dedicated wifeliness?

Where is the appetizer to set before my weary provider; the loving "tell me about *your* day, dear"; the "why don't you put up your feet and read the newspaper while I add the finishing touches to tonight's meal?" I look down at my apron pocket, flapped open where it was pulled from the seams a week (or was it a month?) before. I don't need a mirror to know what the rest of me looks like! Lover, friend—where has she gone?

Our simple reality is this: We come together at a point in the day when we both are depleted. We seem to need each other most when we have the least to give. My ideal would be to greet him with wifely devotion; instead I come to him with needs he is unable to meet.

Can I accept the fact that no one can meet another's needs all of the time? Can I release Dave, release myself, from that expectation? Can I acknowledge that there are times, even in the best relationships, when each individual must rely on his own resources —that no matter how good our intentions, 5:30 P.M. may be such a time for us?

At the heart of our expectations for another is probably the hope that we will find in him what is lacking in ourselves; that when alone we are not enough, we can through another become whole. Yet we must all, at some point, come to grips with the reality that in a certain sense we are alone with ourselves. "There is no one living who has not endured the sharp sorrow of separateness at one time or another. We are our only tenant. What we do with this realization depends upon how at ease we are with the tenant inside.[9]

Having accepted our separateness, we can release the other person and, in so doing, take a giant step toward a healthy relationship. The German poet Rainer Maria Rilke refers to this kind of relationship as "two solitudes that protect and touch and greet each other."[10]

Dave cannot meet all my needs nor can I meet all his needs— only God has promised to do that. To acknowledge that is liberating.

And through my cloud of weariness shines a slender ray of objectivity—a warm meal will go a long way toward carrying us through the final "wind-down" with the children. Life will be an entirely different matter from the other side of 7 P.M.!

151

FOUND WEEKEND

"Goodbye, Daddy." "Bye, Mommy." At last we're off—just Dave and me.

My mind is still whirling. Did I put clean pajamas on the changing table for Jonathan? Were the mealtime instructions clear? Did we leave a number where we can be reached? This has been a trying week, with Jonathan constantly into everything, David and Kimberly at each other continually. A tense, tired, even reluctant me sits back to worry about the children, the house, and vague undefined concerns as we head off for a lost weekend. Is it worth it?

We arrive at our ocean-front motel, make leisurely preparations for the evening, and drive to a dinner theater. After eating our fill from a sumptuous buffet we settle in for the evening entertainment. I can almost feel the tension dissolve, the tightness ease. My conditioned responses are now under control—no longer must I suppress an urge to hoard crackers to stuff in a baby's mouth, scan the crowd to account for my young. Hours and miles removed from routine responsibilities I am finally able to shift gears, unwind, and give myself fully to being Dave's wife!

It *is* good to get away. When was the last time I dressed in leisure (my purpose solely to please Dave) without little ones trying on my jewelry, walking off in my shoes, persistently questioning each detail of my toilette? When was the last time we talked, looking each other in the eyes, without interruption, no ceiling on our time?

It is good to see Dave apart from his work preoccupation—no rush, no hurry. Transported into a totally supportive atmosphere, we talk and listen open-endedly, significantly more satisfying than our "on the run" conversations. I like how he responds to me, how I see myself through his eyes—not a housewife, not a mother, but every inch a woman.

It is amazing really, how removed I feel from it all—the children, household responsibilities, schedules . . . Out of sight and out of mind! For a span of time, removed from "yesterday," isolated from "tomorrow," we are simply this—friends and lovers. I nestle in closer to Dave. My present enjoyment is enhanced by anticipation. I have twenty-four round full hours ahead—alone with Dave!

WHO ARE MY CHILDREN?

From the window I see the children at play, going through their pantomimes of adult activity: David, the father; Kimberly, the mother; Jonathan, of course, the baby. In and out of the playhouse they go; over to the sandbox "to work"; back "home" again; Jonathan compliantly submitting to each directive with a docileness uncharacteristic of real life. It jolts me to chance upon my young about their play—thinking their own thoughts, exercising their will, functioning independently of me. I, who once held them within me, who felt their every stirring, who was their single connection with life, see them now as strangers, occupied in plots and plans of their own making. I feel anew the startling sense of separateness that accompanies this awareness that my children are growing up to grow away.

It should not come as a surprise. From their entrance into this world they have been moving away; birth itself was the first in a series of breakaways. And while I feel an emotional resistance to this, most of what I'm investing in their lives is deliberately aimed toward this end—making them independent of us. "I can do it myself" is a reassuring indication they are headed in the right direction; "I need my privacy" is a healthy sign of their emerging personal identity. Their thoughts and plans are filled with becoming an adult, accommodating the world to their ever changing status. Much of their talk concerns the same:

Kimberly: I wonder what it feels like to be a mother.
Me: You do?
Kimberly: Yes. Do you ever wonder what it feels like to be a little girl?
Me: No, because I once was a little girl.

Kimberly: Did you like it?

Me: Yes.

Kimberly: Do you wish you could be a little girl again?

Me: Sometimes.

Kimberly: Oh no—remember? Spankings!

Children living in a world where adults are their measure . . . Little wonder, their preoccupation with growing up!

We assist them in this process knowing fully that each step carries them a little further from us, that all we pour into them is directed toward strengthening them to leave us. And I, a novice in "letting go," accept each break-away—the first bottle, the first baby-sitter, the first day of school—as an exercise, a training for the bigger things—the first date, the first license, the first year in college, leaving home . . .

Even as I deal with the specifics of daily release, I know in my heart it is but an acknowledgment of what is in fact already a given—that my children are not possessions, but a trust put in my keeping. As a steward of this God-given trust, I am responsible for their nurture. This "trust vs. possession" concept has a signally liberating aspect: I am responsible to God for my investment in my children, but they alone exercise their will and in the final analysis they alone must account to God for their actions. I am accountable for how I *deal* with their behavior, but *they* are accountable for their behavior.

Who are my children? God-given trusts. Children of God, committed into my keeping, yet ultimately accountable to Him. My day-to-day acts of relinquishment are only tokens of an even deeper release—the renunciation of ownership by committing these trusts back into the care of the Giver, their Heavenly Father.

6

*"Growth of A Soul"** *

"You sought to put us in touch with our Creator through your example and guidance. Even in my times of darkest doubts the integration of your faith into everyday living has offered a convincing evidence of its reality."

* Hudson Taylor's biography.

THE BEGINNING

I'm cleaning up the kitchen; Kimberly walks in and announces, "I asked Jesus into my heart. Did He come in?"

I try not to appear jolted but I'm thinking, she's so young. She doesn't know what it's all about.

She persists. "Did He come in?"

I stall. "When did you ask Him, honey?"

"Last night when you and David were talking. I asked Him in a whisper. Do you think maybe He didn't hear?"

"Oh yes, I'm sure He heard." But I know I have not answered her question. I wish her father was here.

I ask more questions to test her four-year-old understanding. It's so limited. I can't help but compare when David asked Jesus into his heart at six years of age. He had a basic understanding of sin, his need for forgiveness, and the blood of Christ shed for the cleansing of sin. I feel let down. I steer her away from this subject; I must think this through. O God, grant me the wisdom to respond rightly to Kimberly.

Thoughts turn over in my mind all day. She is responding fully to the amount of light she has been given. Can I deny her the satisfaction of acknowledging what is, however limited, the beginning of a process?

Late afternoon. I sit on the porch swing reading. Kimberly comes up and rests her elbows on my knees. "Mommy, *did* Jesus come into my heart when I asked him?"

"Yes, Kimberly. He did hear you and He did come into your heart. When Daddy comes home we'll all kneel together as a family and thank Jesus."

Kimberly skips off. The tears I fight sting my eyes. Yes, she has responded fully to her present light.

I think back on a little girl of five kneeling with her family in the living room. I can see the pattern I was finger-tracing on the chair as vividly as if it were before me now. This moment was the result of my repeated request to "help me ask Jesus into my heart." Did I have a full understanding of the issues involved? No. But it was a beginning. From that point on I was conscious of an added dimension of responsibility. What I did, who I was, mattered to God. This awareness was undoubtedly encouraged by my parents but it was definitely recognized by me.

In the following years unquestioningly I absorbed and accepted matters of faith. The first challenge to my faith occurred early in high school when I saw Christians portrayed unsympathetically in a play at summer stock theater. I began to question:

—If I had grown up in a non-Christian home would I have mirrored the beliefs of my parents?

—Since I base my faith on the Bible, what confidence do I have that it is a reliable historical document?

—What distinguishes the Bible from other religious documents?

Thus began my covert search. I finally miserably admitted my doubts to Mother, who encouraged me to discuss my questions. I had reached the point where I had to work through for myself that which I had before accepted at another's word.

After wrestling with doubts for one disturbing year without any significant resolution, a new question came into play. My brother puts it this way: What is your doubting posture? Is it with your fist shaking in God's face saying, "I dare you to show me," or on your knees, with arms outstretched, saying, "God, if there is a God, show me?"

I determined, on the basis of what I had observed and experienced, to assume the second posture. I renewed my commitment to Christ. Yet deep within me, unspoken and nagging, was the fear that what I believed, while true, held an embarrassingly weak defense from an intellectual point of view.

Four years later I read C. S. Lewis's *Mere Christianity*. Clearly and probingly he began his case based on his journey out of atheism. I would read and say, "Oh yes, but . . ." And he would go on to say, "Yes, but . . ." and work through my question. On

159

we went, he in effect taking me by the hand, answering my questions one by one. And he went further—down roads I hadn't yet traveled, answering questions I hadn't thought to ask.

That was a turning point in my life. I could symbolically hold my head high, believing now not only with my heart but with my mind Christianity to be the most valid world view.

What had complicated my quest was that spiritual realities cannot be test-tube-proven, for that which cannot be seen or touched cannot be subjected to the scientific test. I wanted *proof* but I was dealing with evidence.

Therefore, it became a matter of considering evidences. For me, that involved taking seriously evidence which might lead to something other than Christianity. Finally coming to the conclusion that the evidence overwhelmingly pointed to the truth of Christianity, I found that acceptance of the same ultimately involved a step of faith. Not a leap into darkness based on blind faith, but a step based on thorough consideration of evidences.

I believe with all my heart that once that step of faith is taken, there are experiential proofs in everyday living.

> It is obvious that were we to insist on the proof first, then faith, order in our daily lives, organized life as we know it would grind to a screeching halt. And, since life together among people is possible only by faith, as we act out trust in other people, it should not seem odd that the same law applies to our life with God.[1]

Having a reversed order in my life of acceptance first (as a child), then questions, I had the distinct advantage through my time of doubting of having previously experienced the reality of Christ to some degree.

My process has made me sympathetic to those who find it difficult to accept that which cannot be measured physically. To some it may be enough to believe someone has said "this is truth," but it was not enough for me.

But I take literally Jeremiah 29:13: "And you will seek Me and find Me, when you search for Me with all your heart."[2] And I would pass on to those who sincerely desire to know the truth

John Stott's prayer for the honest seeker. I believe it to be the beginning point in the way of truth.

O God, if You exist (and I am not sure if You do), and if You can hear this prayer (and I do not know if You can), I want You to know that I am an honest seeker after the truth. My mind is open; I am willing to believe. My will is surrendered. I am ready to obey. Teach me the truth. Show me if Jesus is Your Son and the Savior of the world. And if You bring conviction to my mind, I promise that I will accept Him as my Savior and follow Him as my Lord. Amen.[3]

ALONE WITH GOD

John Wesley's prayer room. I study the postcard before me. The room is small, starkly furnished with a bench, a chair, and a desk. On the desk is a candle and a Bible. The words written on the back of the card never fail to move me: "This room where John Wesley prayed and read his Bible each morning and night has been called the Power House of Methodism. He said, 'Here then I am, far from the busy ways of men. I sit down alone—only God is here.' "[4]

I have kept this card in my Bible ever since my visit to the John Wesley home in London, England. I was a college student caught up with sightseeing, shopping, and glamorous evenings out. The dreary tours of historic homes and monuments I simply endured. So with reluctance I dutifully accompanied my parents to "another old home." I distinctly remember lagging behind the rest of the group, who appeared fascinated by the mechanical recitation of the guide. As I approached the prayer room, my group descended the narrow stairs.

I stood before that tiny room that was such a sacred meeting place between God and man. An overwhelming longing for greater spiritual reality welled up within me. I sensed there was more to the Christian life than I was experiencing. But as I looked at this bleak room so removed from action and excitement, I was struck with the contrast between my desires and God's way of dealing with man. I wanted miracles performed by a Houdini God. I wanted to skip the conditions and get on with the promises. I longed for mountaintop experiences. God insisted I learn to walk before trying to scale the heights. I sought the benefits of the Christian life. God wanted me to seek after *Him*. I wanted it all

162

now. But God knew I required a process made up of just plain living. Living that included stretching experiences, and ordinary daily routines; progress and setbacks; forgiving and being forgiven; joy and heartaches. In a moment of reverence and humility, I relinquished my false expectations and pledged to spend more time alone with God. On my way out, I bought this postcard as a reminder of my vow.

Many years have since passed. I can't help but compare *my* places of prayer with John Wesley's prayer room! Long ago I set aside my dream of a cloistered place of retreat. No door separates me from the children's constant interruptions. Yet I have staked off several spots to be my places of encounter with God.

Through trial and error I have come up with some procedures that make this time with God meaningful to me. With my Bible, monthly planning calendar, notebook, and cup of coffee, I settle in for a daily time of Bible reading:[5] After asking God to help me understand His Word, I ask myself questions about the reading: What is the main point? What do I learn of God? What insight am I given into myself or a life situation? What is required of me in response to this reading? Then I turn the things I have learned into prayers of thanksgiving, confession, petition, or adoration.

During this time, if I start thinking about things I need to do during the day, I write them down. If I suddenly remember a meeting I'm to attend, I place it on my calendar. This is not a time to be segregated from the mundane matters of daily living, it is a time to strengthen and equip me *for* them. "In our era, the way of holiness must necessarily pass through the way of action."[6] Unconventional? Perhaps. But it works for me.

It was the symbolic impact of John Wesley's prayer room that made me aware of my need for time alone with God. This postcard is a visual reminder of that fact. But my experience has taught me that spiritual reality is not dependent on tangible props. In the physical sense I have no place "far from the busy ways of men" (or children). Rather, in the maelstrom of life, with a heart open to my Maker, I can declare, "Here then I am, far from the busy ways of men, I sit down alone—only God is here."

ANXIETY

It all happened at once. My junior year of college—my neat little world, with its answers and formulas for every conceivable life situation, collapsed along with its easy answers. They weren't sufficient to explain the three crises that converged on my life. Dave's mother died from cancer, leaving four children, two still at home. A loved one was forced into a marriage at the age of fifteen. A business venture of Father's was totaled by financial reverses. Each situation shared common ground—the consistent claiming prayers of godly people and irreversible damages—nothing gained but pain to all involved. In each situation a positive solution would have brought witness to God's power.

Up to this point my world view was adequate for my experience. The troublesome questions were theoretical. They did not affect my everyday life. For the first time I was faced with realities bigger than my world view.

Oh, I had witnessed suffering. But somehow I had come up with an idea which had not been contradicted by my experience: "If I do my best to live a good Christian life, if I cover each problem with prayer, God will spare me life's tragedies. Certainly I will face trials and testing (necessary for growth), but in the final analysis God will deliver those who love and serve Him." And they lived happily ever after . . .

Now I was witnessing Christians with faith and experience far beyond mine go through situations which had no happy ending. The bottom was pulled out from under me.

My first response was grief. Grief for those I loved. Grief for the loss of the child me. Then *fear*. How could I—how could anyone be safe in a world that was no respecter of persons? I searched for

164

promises and formulas which could secure for me some guaranties. I could find biblical examples of men whom God had delivered from harm. But I could find no promise that *I* would be spared life's ills. Did God deliver Paul, Stephen, Peter . . . ?

In the passing of time the specific fears subsided to be replaced by something new—anxiety. Too shadowy even to deal with, but there nonetheless, evidencing itself in a vague, gnawing sadness. Sadness with a world that promised nothing, that shot risk through even the happiest moments. I recognized what I felt to be inconsistent with biblical promise and command.

> For God hath not given us the spirit of fear; but of power, and of love, and of a sound mind.[7]

> Be anxious for nothing . . . And the peace of God, which surpasses all comprehension, shall guard your hearts and your minds in Christ Jesus.[8]

The desire to reconcile my fears with what I understood to be spiritual truth was the prime mover in my endeavor to come to grips with living in a world without guaranties. I worked through these five points:

—When God designed man with the freedom to choose Him, it allowed man the freedom to reject Him as well.

—Man did. And out of kilter with His Creator, man was incapable of living life rightly or fully.

—Thus a broken world. Not God's ideal for man, but permitted, to allow man free will.

—As part of this broken world we share in the sorrows of the family of man. Biblical accounts show that God sometimes intervenes—but not always.

—The promise is the hope of eternal union with God—perfect wholeness.

But what about *now*? We cannot know the mind of God fully, but some things He has made clear.

He loves us. It is repeatedly stated in His written word and demonstrated ultimately through Christ. He cares about our happiness on earth.

Have you and I got a master we can trust? Do we ask first of all to be allowed to examine and approve of the scheme? The Apostle Paul admitted the limitations of his own understanding.

"Now we know in part," he said. "Now we see through a glass darkly." But he was absolutely sure of his Master. He never said, I know why this is happening. He said, "I know whom I have believed. I am absolutely sure that nothing can separate us from the love of God."[9]

While we are not promised guaranties, He has promised to take us by the hand and walk through every valley with us. *He* is our sufficiency.

As for those situations so tragic, so senseless, God will redeem even the bad, so to speak, making it work for the good.[10] God can pick up the broken pieces and use them to reconstruct something even greater than man could have imagined.

It really seems to come down to two realities, the outward circumstances of our lives, and spiritual reality that transcends these circumstances. This is so clearly illustrated in Corrie ten Boom's observation of life at the concentration camp:

Life at Ravensbruck took place on two separate levels mutually impossible. One, the observable, external life, grew every day more horrible. The other, the life we lived with God, grew daily better truth upon truth, glory upon glory.[11]

These, I believe, are the facts. But the integrating of these facts into my experience is a process that has gone on for some years. That continues even now. That involves faith in the most practical sense of the word. Stepping out. Taking risks. Living life fully —knowing whatever that may involve, God is enough. A growing optimism based on the acceptance of life's given hand in hand with God has gradually erased anxiety. I still have fears that lift their nasty heads and leer at me. I don't like it—but it brings me humbly before God saying, "God, help. I need You. I pray that Perfect Love will cast out this fear today, for this moment." That's all. That's enough.

166

The adventurous life is not one exempt from fear, but, on the contrary, one that is lived in full knowledge of fears of all kinds, one in which we go forward in spite of our fears.[12]

Thirteen years have passed since that crucial year. I would never have willed one of those crises. But I can testify to how God has redeemed each of those situations—taking the broken pieces and putting them together for good. And as it forced me to draw on God's resources, I can witness to the goodness of a loving God. It is with that confidence that I make the following contract with God:

What I have to do is to put my signature at the foot of a blank page on which I will accept whatever God wishes to write.

I cannot predict what He will put on this blank contract as my life proceeds—but I give my signature today.[13]

FATHER, FORGIVE . . .

It has been one of those very special evenings. Everything worked together to make it so. The night drive up to Mountain Lake Sanctuary. Making our approach on foot to Bok Tower, through the iron gates, across the moat, the stars and moon our only lights. Swinging open the massive brass doors leading into the castle room of the tower. Our many-storied ascent in the tiny elevator. The view from the tower window, lights scattered randomly across the countryside below us.

The occasion? A shared listening adventure—Benjamin Britten's *War Requiem*, written for the dedication service of the rebuilt St. Michael's Cathedral of Coventry.

What was going through our minds as we heard the somber music of the Latin Mass interspersed with the foxhole poetry about the futility of war by a young pacifist soldier who was killed two weeks before the signing of the armistice in 1918?

Were we thinking of the rows of white markers photographed on both sides of the album jacket—poignant reminders of the war dead?

Were we responding to the dignity, the aching majesty of the music? Its final victorious resolve?

Or were we reliving the first performance of the *Requiem* in the rebuilt cathedral? How many of the survivors gathered that day were reminded of the nine-hour continuous hail of incendiary and high-explosive bombs some twenty years before. How it reduced the town center to rubble, the cathedral to charred ruins.

As I listened, two words kept coming to my mind: FATHER, FORGIVE. Words engraved in stone behind a cross of charred roof timbers, enshrined in the forecourt of the rebuilt cathedral placed on the site of the former high altar. FATHER, FOR-GIVE . . . I think of the people gathered to witness the reconstruction of these ruins, symbolic of man's indestructible spirit. A miracle indeed, to sustain the loss of loved ones, one's place, one's center of worship. To put together the broken pieces. Ah, yes, a miracle. But a forgiving spirit . . . Without a doubt the greatest miracle of all. True forgiveness—a gift of grace, not the result only of human effort. To forgive *is* divine.

So few of us will be called upon to forgive at that level. Thank God. Yet we are called upon to forgive at whatever level of experience we find ourselves. It should be enough that our Teacher commanded us to forgive, but like all God's laws, there is a good reason behind it.

I think back on my strange lesson in forgiving, so pale contrasted to that charred cross, but a lesson in forgiving nonetheless.

I had reached a point in my life where I was having difficulty coping with an increasing sense of dissatisfaction with myself. It came down to some significant gaps between what I wanted to be and what I was. In retrospect, I can see that some of these gaps were related to the stress of my life situation—babies, the inability to schedule anything, exhaustion. But the reality, all the same, was a flagging self-esteem. In my attempt to come to terms with my life, I realized I had to either raise my performance or lower my standards. This involved taking a hard look at the real me (whoever that was) in an endeavor to determine if what I was trying to do or be was because it was right for me, or because it was "expected" of me.

This was pretty heavy stuff. Guess who got in on the act? My parents! As I began to distinguish what was authentic for me, I began to resent what I considered their past attempts to mold me into their idea of what I should be. There was quite a gap between what I perceived *their* ideal to be—a cool, controlled, balanced lady—and the spontaneous me, so given to ideas that exceeded my energy. I unearthed some hurts that went back to my early college days when I felt they underestimated my standards or exhibited lack of trust in some of my choices. I resisted some of their expectations which *I* didn't consider important, yet continued to make my measure. Housekeeping would be a good example. Mother's standards can best be illustrated in how she scrubbed a floor—down on her hands and knees, Ajax in one hand, hairpin within easy reach ("For those corners!"). I, too, loved a clean, ordered home; I just had a different definition of cleanliness and order. I began to collect evidences of their failure to affirm me in areas I considered important. I developed quite a case!

At points I was genuinely misunderstood; in some areas there was a legitimate difference in point of view; in other areas I simply was unwilling to accept certain realities about myself. Had I been more secure at that time in who I was, I could have treated it just that objectively. Instead, I focused on my parents' mishandling of certain situations to the exclusion of recognizing their overwhelmingly positive input. As I dwelt on my collection of hurts, I felt a growing resentment toward my parents.

It just happened that during this period of time I began to read Paul Tournier's *The Healing of Persons*. How I devoured each word. I could see through many of his illustrations subtle ways in which my parents contributed to some of the frustrations I was experiencing. I "amened" him with the turn of each page. Until page 161. The words leaped out at me: "ONE MUST ACCEPT ONE'S PARENTS."[14] At the risk of doing an injustice to Dr. Tournier, I'll attempt to expand his reasoning.

> We have no right to expect perfection from anyone. Maturity involves coming to grips with our given. Our parents are part of our given, along with all *their* given.
>
> Part of accepting our parents, therefore, involves accepting all they have passed on to us. The hang-ups along with the "inheritance."
>
> At the heart of acceptance lies forgiveness. Forgiving where they may have failed us by what they are or are not, what they have done or left undone.

This spoke right to me. Rather than be resentful of inadequacies or hurts for which I was holding my parents responsible, I had to accept those very things as part of my given—along with my race, my sex, and the shape of my nose. This involved a total

170

acceptance of my parents and forgiving wherever I believed (rightly or wrongly) myself to have been wronged. But I was faced with a dilemma. How does one forgive for things done (or not done) unintentionally? To confront my parents at this point, even with forgiveness, could only bring unnecessary hurt over things they would be unable to do anything about.

With an insight that I believe to be from God's Spirit, I determined to forgive through Christ. As each hurt or lack of understanding came into my consciousness, I would bring it before God and release it in an act of forgiveness. The issue was no longer my parents' rightness or wrongness. That was entirely beside the point. Whatever cause of resentment or hurt I found in my heart (regardless how insignificant, how unintentional, or how foolish it seemed even to me) was faced and released through this act of forgiveness.

A process was going on in me which gave me a firsthand insight into the "why" behind God's imperative "forgive." A gentle healing of bruises of the spirit was taking place apart from any effort of my own toward this end. There was no instant miracle. It was just that one day I realized it had been some time since I had felt the need to deal with any resentment. I was conscious of a refreshing wholeness of spirit. And with that came a change of perspective—a new way of seeing things. Petty hurts were replaced with deep understanding that enabled me to see things clearly from my parents' point of view. The doors were flung open for an adult relationship.

What does all this have to do with Coventry? Am I trying to compare my surface scratches with their deep mortal wounds? No! One can't even begin to compare these two situations. That isn't the point at all! The common ground is not the wound, it is the prescription for healing. When we deal with ourselves it is not a matter of comparison. We must simply deal with our level of experience, no matter how insignificant it may seem in the light of another's experience. Resentment resulting from *any* hurt makes us spirit-sick. It poisons the soul. Cripples the spirit. The prescription for healing is always the same—forgiveness. The greatest victory at Coventry was not the magnificent reconstruction of its cathedral. It was the stone-carved inscription, FATHER, FORGIVE, the visual demonstration of a spiritual principle well worth branding on the fleshy tablets of our heart—forgive.

Just as it is easy to overestimate our hurt, it is easy to underestimate our need to forgive. I would even suggest that we may be less inclined to deal with the mild nagging symptoms of the small hurts than the acute symptoms of a major wound. Yet are they any less important for their apparent insignificance? Is it not the little hurts and resentments that tend to fester as they collect in our heart, until we have an infected spirit? Their very insignificance prevents us from locating the hurt and following the prescription.

The survivors at Coventry knew what they were dealing with and what was required for spirit healing. Perhaps with that perspective we might find it in ourselves to do likewise within the sphere of our experience. *Then* we can say with confidence and faith, "Father, forgive us as we have forgiven others."[15]

172

PROBLEMS—INTRUDERS OR FRIENDS?

Vacation . . . Walk to the lighthouse. Waves pound against the sand. The roar of the ocean covers all other sounds, giving me a deceptive sense of isolation. I reflect on all that has happened since the last time I walked this beach. Last year's vacation—the proverbial "lull before the storm" . . .

We returned home to PROBLEMS. Problems that swept over us, that threatened to engulf us. Misrepresentations, deliberate deceptions. After presenting facts where it was demanded, we determined silence to be in the best interest of everyone. Silence that forced us to hoist a heavy burden onto our own shoulders and walk alone. Loneliness threatened to suffocate us. And paranoia . . . What had been said to whom? Of what was said, what was believed? And how would it affect them?

My initial response—withdrawal. Dave's, deep discouragement. But neither were luxuries we could indulge in. We had to go through the motions of normal living—all our strength channeled into one effort—emotional survival. Again and again we'd regain our balance only to be buffeted by a continuation of spin-off problems that threatened to knock us over. Our inner resources exhausted, we were forced to claim from God *His* sufficiency. We read the Apostle James's advice:

> When all kinds of trials and temptations crowd into your lives, my brothers, don't resent them as intruders, but welcome them as friends![16]

Welcome these problems as friends? Could I ever?

Not yet. But we did have to learn to cope in a way that wouldn't allow these problems to dominate our daily living. We attempted to put the problems into the proper perspective by seeing them in relation to things that *really* mattered. What a comfort our children were by their dear uncomplicated presence.

We began to discipline our minds by enforcing ground rules that had served us well in other situations. We subjected all conversation pertaining to the problems to this test: If it has been already thoroughly discussed it must be laid to rest unless there was additional information that altered the situation or insight relevant to the resolve of the problems. (I sneaked in an additional clause—or was crucial to one's peace of mind!) I admit to repeatedly offering questionable relevant insights but some unnecessarily draining discussion was siphoned off by this restraint.

We fought negative thinking patterns by focusing on the positive things that lift the spirit. We began to appreciate Paul's sound advice:

> And now, my friends, all that is true,
> All that is noble,
> All that is just and pure,
> All that is lovable and gracious,
> Whatever is excellent and admirable
> Fill all your thoughts with these things.[17]

In time we began to turn from the question "Why is this happening to us?" to "What can we learn from this?" It was frightening to realize that we could be "so right in our position" but if we allowed our spirits to be poisoned with resentment, we could end up "so wrong." How we dealt with the issue was infinitely more important than the problems themselves. We read on in our "welcome trials as friends" passage:

> Realize that they come to test your faith and to produce in you the quality of endurance. But let the process go on until that endurance is fully developed, and you find you have become men of mature character, men of integrity with no weak spots.
>
> And if, in the process, any of you does not know how to meet any problem, he has only to ask God—who gives generously to all men without making them feel guilty—and

174

he may be quite sure that the necessary wisdom will be given him.[18]

Would we just cope? Or would we go deeper, letting the process go on, strengthening the weak spots? We determined to submit ourselves to the refiner's fire and allow God to put this situation to good use in our lives. We turned a corner, as reflected in my journal at that time:

Life goes on—interrupted by problems, struggles, and then resolve. But we are richer for the struggle. Lessons are learned, insights gained that would never be ours through tranquillity. And even through the rough times seasons change, birds sing, babies smile, a letter arrives, a pleasant phone call is made, a compliment is received, an undeserved rose blooms, children laugh and play, the house envelops us with its charm and warmth . . . God is here. In our hearts His Spirit heals.

Can I welcome the trials and temptations of this past year as friends? Yes. I have ceased to ask why or to look for some redeeming reason to justify the damages. I have rested that in God's hands. I only know that I can genuinely thank God for the good He has wrought in our lives through this situation. "The Enemy had probably intended this incident for bad, but the Lord as usual used it for good in our lives."[19]

Through the months of struggle, a song of Andrae Crouch has become our growing testimony and confidence for future testings.

I've had many tears and sorrows;
I've had questions for tomorrow;
There've been times I didn't know right from wrong;
But in ev'ry situation God gave blessed consolation
That my trials come to only make me strong.

I've been to lots of places,
And I've seen a lot of faces;
There've been times I felt so all alone;
But in my lonely hours yes, those precious lonely hours,
Jesus let me know that I was His own.

175

I thank God for the mountains,
And I thank Him for the valleys;
I thank Him for the storms He brought me through;
For if I'd never had a problem,
I wouldn't know that He could solve them,
I'd never know what faith in God could do.

Through it all,
Through it all
Oh I've learned to trust in Jesus,
I've learned to trust in God.
Through it all,
Through it all
Oh I've learned to depend upon His Word.[20]

CREATE IN ME A CLEAN HEART

I am soul-weary. I have been wrapped up in *my* projects, *my* plans, *my* schedule. Insensitive to the needs of people around me, indifferent to God, I suddenly see myself for what I am—just plain full of myself.

Things have been going so well, I didn't realize what was happening. Daily I tip my hat to God, "And the top of the morning to You," then go my merry way. I have been busy, happy, fulfilled. Until all of a sudden everything has gone flat. In my total absorption with myself, I have left no room for God. Full of self, I feel empty.

I know what is needed to put things in order again. Confession. I must come before God and confess all those things that separate me from Him. The selfishness . . . the indifference . . . the pride . . .

How I resist confession—reserve it for the "big things." "I'm not so bad. What blatant sins have I committed?" Yet, I know differently. My own experience has taught me that my "sins of the spirit" separate me from God, just as surely as the more overt "sins of the flesh." That only through confession, full and specific, can I experience again the presence of God.

In the process I'm discovering some releasing side benefits of confession. Paul Tournier says, "Christian confession leads to the same psychological liberation as do the best psychoanalytical techniques."[21] As we confess everything in our field of consciousness other repressed memories return to consciousness. As the One to whom we are responsible forgives us, we experience the refreshing presence of God. "Now you must repent and turn to God so that your sins may be wiped out that time after time

177

your soul may know the refreshment that comes from the presence of God."[22]

O Father in heaven, who didst fashion my limbs to serve Thee and my soul to follow hard after Thee, with sorrow and contrition of heart I acknowledge before Thee the faults and failures of the day that is now past. Too long, Father, have I tried Thy patience; too often have I betrayed the sacred trust Thou hast given me to keep; yet Thou art willing that I should come to Thee in lowliness of heart, as now I do, beseeching Thee to drown my transgressions in the sea of Thine own infinite love.[23]

Create in me a clean heart, O God; and renew a right spirit within me. Cast me not away from thy presence; and take not thy holy spirit from me. Restore unto me the joy of thy salvation, and uphold me with thy free spirit.[24] Amen.

SUCCESS

What is success? There seem to be almost as many definitions as people. How to succeed in life is the subject of hundreds of books, each complete with a full set of directions. History repeats itself again and again as mankind looks to power, wealth, knowledge, prestige, or fame as a measure of success. As we witness those who have succeeded without making a success of their lives, we have been forced to look deeper for answers: Loving and being loved? Self-fulfillment? Realization of personal potential? Is *that* it? It is unbearable to think one could come to the end of life—having invested so much into the business of living—only to realize one has not made a success of living after all.

Paul Tournier speaks to the question of success in his book *The Adventure of Living*.

> The will of God: that is the key to our problem. God has a purpose, and it will be realized also through the failures we must face in obedience.
>
> God has a purpose: the entire Bible proclaims this. What matters is that His plan should be understood and fulfilled. So, in the light of the Bible, the problem is shifted onto new ground. The question is no longer whether one is succeeding or failing but whether one is fulfilling God's purpose or not, whether one is adventuring with Him or against Him.
>
> What is success and what is failure? The answer of the Bible is "What is the will of God? Are you obeying Him?"[25]

The will of God. Yes, *this* is it. I do not need to be convinced. The predominant thread running through my experience is an increasing recognition of my need for God—a growing dependency on what He has to say about everyday living.

But to *know* God's will, that is another matter. Does God speak in a voice audible to man? Write His oracles across the walls to be read by man? Send visions? How can I *know* God's will for my life?

Some things are spelled out in the Bible. Specific commandments. The guiding principles of love. Applicable to *all* Christians. As I meditate on God's word, allowing time for my thoughts to be guided by God, a significant change takes place. I begin to see things from *God's* point of view. I have, in a sense, His mind within me.

But what about those things *not* clearly spelled out in the Bible? This is where God's guidance must come in. "Show me now thy way, that I may know thee . . . And he said, My *presence* shall go with thee, and I will give thee rest."[26]

Catherine Marshall deals with guidance in *Beyond Ourselves:* "The promise that God can guide us is the clear teaching of Scripture both in its total sweep and in its specific promises. This scriptural teaching rests on three pillars:

1. God has all wisdom, hence knows the past and the future and what is best for His children.
2. that He is a God of Love who cares about the individual enough to want to direct him right.
3. that He can communicate with men."[27]

Elisabeth Elliot says, "I would far rather have a guide than the best advice or the clearest set of directions."[28] I must ask God for direction, then be sensitive to all indication of His leading.

These are the teachings. I believe them to be true. But frankly my greatest difficulty comes not so much in the "knowing" as in the "doing." I often do not *feel* like obeying God's commandments or observing His laws of love. But the Bible nowhere speaks in terms of feelings as a requirement for action. It speaks of the will. If I *will* to obey—whether that involves forgiving, loving an unlovable person, submitting to undesirable authority—that is all that matters. I want to *feel* like doing what I am supposed to do. It contradicts my natural bent to act on the basis of the *will*, rather than emotions. But I am promised if I commit myself at the level of the will, the rest will follow.

This book of the law shall not depart out of thy mouth; but thou shalt meditate therein day and night, that thou mayest observe to do according to all that is written therein: for then thou shalt make thy way prosperous, and *then thou shalt have good success.*[29]

If I base my life on principles clearly laid out in Scripture, if I seek God's guidance in the specific concerns of my life, *if* I will to obey God—*then* I will have good success.

O Lord, all things that are in heaven and earth are Thine. I desire to offer myself unto Thee, willingly and freely to be Thine forever . . . in the simplicity of my heart I offer myself unto Thee this day . . .[30]

THE "END"

"Since you have accepted Christ Jesus as Lord, *live* in union with Him."[31]

Acceptance—the *beginning* of a process. Just that. The translating of belief into the daily living level is what the Christian life is all about. I'm so impatient with that process—so eager for "end" results.

The growth of a soul—a process made up of all those things that stretch, expand, chip away, refine—that discipline our souls in the course of everyday living.

> Submit to the discipline of the Father of men's souls, and *learn* how to live.[32]

Could it be that what we call the process, God calls the "end?"

7

A Room of My Own*

"You helped me identify positively with being a woman in a world where there is such uncertainty. I'm discovering life is made up of choices that are not only between good and bad but between good and good, and that these quality-of-life choices have more to do with being a person than being a woman."

---

* Adapted from A Room of One's Own by Virginia Woolf.

LIFE STAGES

I just can't seem to get anything done . . . I have needs to accomplish things beyond the daily routine, but it seems that whatever I set about to do is frustrated by constant demands from children. First it was the urgent physical demands of the infant: night crying, endless feedings, diaper changes. No sooner did I get a full night of sleep than my baby was a toddler, clinging, whining at my ankles. Nothing entertained that baby of mine but my full attention—or so it seemed. His world expanded and so did the territory I had to cover with my safety concerns. At all times I had to know what my toddler-child was doing—touching, tasting, ever stretching the boundaries of his known world.

As the physical demands subsided, the mental demands increased. The more demanding question "Why?" replaced "What's that?" My attempts to adjust tasks to the child's insistence "I can do it myself" were inadequate. The beginning of school has offered the gift of added hours, but these hours are now divided between two more young. I am reaching in three directions at once—three stages of development are going on at the same time.

By now, I know with certainty that these demands and interruptions are all a part of the given of mothering. I must stop saying: when he sleeps through the night, when I stop nursing, when he walks, when he feeds himself, when he starts school—for as long as a child of mine remains in our home, there will be distractions.

This I now accept. But this acceptance was born of a crisis-precipitated insight. It was within the first six months of our first baby's life. He was an intense, semi-colicky baby. When he

184

awakened he "wah-wah-wahed" without letup, building in intensity until a bottle was thrust into his mouth. He sucked so vigorously he would break into a sweat, polishing off his bottle in record-breaking time. When he realized after several dry sucks that his bottle was "all gone," he would cry for several more minutes from sheer disappointment.

I can remember sinking into the living room sofa in exhaustion, looking out the window and watching the world go by. And I'd observe how everything looked the same—as always, the same people walked by the same houses, going to the same places as if nothing had changed at all. Yet everything was so different! I mentally calculated how many years it would be before I would be able to join this world again. Adding the possibility of a couple more babies, I was staggered by my computations.

One neighbor woman in particular became the focus of my attention. She was an attractive woman, probably in her early fifties. Daily she would drive by my window during the 11 A.M. feeding, on her way to a friend's indoor pool for a quick pre-lunch dip. I'd see her reading on her flower-filled deck, sipping a tall cool drink —most likely lemonade clinking with ice cubes, topped with a sprig of mint. Frequently a carload of well-dressed women would pull up to her house. I pictured them sitting in her beautifully appointed living room, engaged in stimulating conversation about a current book or relevant issue. No doubt they were drinking tea from porcelain teacups (purchased on a recent European trip) and eating delicate confections that she had put together in loving leisure.

One day it was brought to my attention that *she* was a mother of five children! From this new data I began to make some deductions. She, too, had walked the floor at night with a crying baby, had heated formulas and worked a stubborn bubble from a distressed infant—and watched the world go by. Five times! And she survived! Now she has hours open to her that she must not have had for years.

My musing began to take the shape of one valuable insight— there are stages in life. The years with children may be roughly a twenty-year stage. But I've had twenty-six years when I assumed the responsibility for no one but myself. Add twenty years and I'll be forty-six with years ahead to enjoy activities of my choosing without the responsibility of children. And then in a moment of further insight (not typical of those early months of mothering) I could see that even within that twenty-year period, there would be a further breakdown of stages—the years with children in the home; the transitional years as the children one by one begin grade school; then there would be the day when they all would be in school; and finally the break-away years as they went off into the world themselves. (So transported was I by my thoughts, I almost wept for my adult children!) I could see that each stage would offer new options.

Having gained some sense of the whole, I came to a basic acceptance that there are limitations unique to each stage, that I cannot do everything at once, that life involves choices.

I am presently learning that I'm a much happier person when I choose activities, in fact a life-style, supportive to my life situation. Unfortunately, there is no pat formula that will spell out exactly what these choices should be; there are too many variables. Just when I think I've arrived at the perfect life style for my present situation, something always comes up to alter my present situation. But in the selective process, through trial and error, some patterns are emerging which I think I could call Principles Which Seem to Work for Me. (How's that for a decisive statement to the world!)

1. Keep in mind the bigger picture. I'm talking about an attitude, an approach toward the details of everyday living. The specifics in and of themselves can seem so insignificant—even demeaning unless seen in their proper context. I think Gladys Hunt puts her finger on this in *MS Means Myself:*

> We tend to ask such small questions about our role in life. For instance, students ask me, Do you like housework? I suppose they ask that because it represents the epitome of slavery to them and because they seem unaware that any commitment has its less exciting moments. I never ask myself that question. It is irrelevant. It is akin to asking a student if she likes to study, or a man if he likes to drive to work. Housework is only a small part of a larger picture I am paint-

ing with my life. Does an artist like cleaning her brushes? I don't discuss the pleasure of housework; I do it. And yet, questions like these often mark the small talk of women. Are we that confused?

Do I like housework? And who will be influenced by my life? There are two different kinds of questions. If I answer the latter, I may more gladly accept the former. Our problem is that we often do not even know when questions are not of the same value. Hence, we have difficulty fitting short-range goals into long-range satisfactions.[1]

2.   Make a point of choosing some interests that can be based in the home. My interest in the decorative arts can range from planning the color scheme of an entire room to setting the breakfast room table. I play at growing roses—which means from eight bushes I consider myself fortunate to keep one bud vase going. If determination means anything, I'll be known city-wide for my homemade yeast rolls—someday. I will never exhaust the possibilities—possibilities which are not limited to those of homemaking. I suppose some women will never get any more excited over decorating than I will over sewing. But I've seen women edit math textbooks, practice an oboe for a metropolitan symphony, prepare canvases for quarterly art shows—at home.

My real boundaries are not the physical boundaries of my house, but boundaries of self. Tied to three young children in a small town amidst the orange groves of central Florida, I shop in the most luxurious stores in the world—through my ever increasing stack of catalogues. I am stimulated by insights from the penetrating minds of "the greats" from books checked out of our local library. On television I have watched Thornton Wilder's *Our Town*, have seen André Previn direct the Pittsburgh Symphony, and have had a better view of Tchaikovsky's *Nutcracker* than I did at the opera house in Chicago. The size of my world is up to me!

3.   Simplify! While I love to set the table with our china and silver, roll out butterballs, place tiny silver salts and peppers at each place setting, and light the candles for a several-course company dinner, I find that unless I can plan each detail well in ad-

vance, it simply isn't worth it for the people who have to live with me. A simpler menu and table setting works better for us all—and still is lovely by candlelight. I'm even leaning more toward having people in just for dessert—after the children are tucked in. This same principle can be applied in almost every other area. And I find the more efficiently I manage the routines of my life the more time and energy I have to invest in the extra-special things.

4. Establish realistic nap times and bedtimes for the children —and enforce them. Even the children anticipate their play-nap as a time to get off by themselves and "work" without interruption. Their consistent and reasonable bedtime has offered Dave and me some guiltless evenings out, knowing our sleeping children have been lovingly tucked in.

5. Make innovative use of those time blocks when I can get away. The extreme of this principle was my weekly 6:30 A.M. tennis game "under lights" with another young mother equally eager to get away from the house. We were falsely accused of spending more time at the local Koffee Kup than playing tennis—but the whole package deal did amazing things for our world view. Dave was the originator of this principle. Tied down with two preschoolers, and carrying number three, I was bemoaning my present state of affairs. Dave caught me up short by pointing out that during the entire time I was complaining he was home and willing to take care of the children. I left the house right then and there and walked downtown feeling much like J. J. M. M. W. G. Dupree's mother in A. A. Milne's poem "Disobedience," who was "last seen wandering vaguely quite of her own accord."[2] That was a start. Since then I consult with Dave, "Will you be watching a Saturday afternoon game?" and I willingly accept what the house will look like when I return from my "vague wanderings."

6. Seek out supportive adult contact. I find I need this. Again, only through experimentation have I found what outside activities actually do uplift me, and for those, I find the occasional cost of a baby-sitter more than worth it.

Oh yes, there are days when I can't complete the most basic routines, and there are times I don't have the energy to go through with my carefully made plans. But one thing I know, I'm a long way from those days on my living room couch, watching the world go by!

SAYING NO

Well, it happened again—I said no and they didn't understand. They couldn't accept that while I didn't have a conflict, it would still be too much for me to handle. I'm observing an interesting thing: When I'm pregnant and then caring for my newborn baby, people have a deep respect—even awe—for my time. I'm virtually left alone. Nothing is expected of me. But somewhere well into the first year of baby's life, things change. It's as if some unnamed committee has been formed; members are drawn from each major organization, and from a mutual consensus declare, "She's ready!" The phone begins to ring, and eager to be reinstated in the adult world, I begin to take on too much. It's the many little things that begin to clutter my life, draining me more than one or two focused efforts.

How do I deal with the responsibility I feel to support the church and community institutions that are designed to support me? Do I have the right to draw from these institutions without supporting them with my efforts? I hear, "Someone has to do it." "Everybody is so busy." And even if I can justify my uninvolvement, is that what I want? So I pick and choose; take on too much, back off a little. But in all that I do I feel I could have done better without so many distractions. And it seems ironic that what I'm doing for my children often so drains me that I'm less than I should be with my children.

How can I cut through the clutter of my life and determine what is important? I know that not only are my efforts needed, but I have needs to give something beyond the perpetuation of my own "show." Yet because of the many demands made, I am forced to develop some sort of selective process to determine which functions I should involve myself in and then to what

189

degree. It comes down to weighing the needs of various organizations with my interests and abilities. The answer is rarely clearcut. Usually it requires difficult choices. Since I can't do everything, I must turn down one good thing to do another good thing. These choices are not static either. My life situation is constantly in a state of flux.

Yet out of my trial and error some helpful insights have emerged. I must avoid comparisons. There are far too many variables to make comparisons valid. That someone else is doing more than I means neither that I'm inadequate nor that she is overextended. To each man his own! Others may challenge me or push their organizational needs. That is their right. But it is my right to make my choices for personal reasons and after a simple explanation, put the matter to rest. At the same time I need to be open to re-evaluating my choices. Have I taken on too much, has something come up that I should consider? Rigidity precludes growth.

I feel so deeply that in this area where we women share mutual pressures we need to rise up and support each other, rather than undermine one another with lack of understanding and criticism.

SELF-ACTUALIZATION

Exercising of gifts. Realization of potential. Self-actualization. Words, words, words . . . Words flung out far and wide, winging their way into the minds of the woman of today. Regardless of our outward response, there lies deep within our hearts the fear that in committing ourselves to our homes and families we may in some way emerge less of a person. Is it possible to make a top-priority commitment to the home and still come out a whole person? How easily my goals shift from the tangible, the measurable, to simply getting through another day. I make efforts to develop in concrete areas but often they are washed out for whole periods of time by pressing family demands or even at best are subject to interruption.

Take the harp. I finally made some progress—a technique is mastered, new music is learned—then I have baby number three. Now I only touch the harp to chord out songs or work up old music for special occasions. No growth. One year later I resume my lessons, then leave on a month-long vacation. I work at my music again. More interruptions: long-anticipated house guests, calendar accelerated by Christmas activities, an epidemic of chicken pox. All three at once. Even when I am on a practice schedule, it is interrupted by Jonathan climbing on the harp (a great adaptation of a slide to his way of thinking). I'm frustrated by my feeble results. Around those I admire in these areas, I'm a pathetic amateur. ("How are you coming on the harp? When are you going to play for us?" I smile and answer noncommittally, "Oh, it's coming along," and wonder if they'd like to hear me play "Greensleeves" again.) Perhaps I could preserve my dignity, eliminate my frustration altogether if I'd simply give these things up for the time being.

What is the answer to this whole area of self-actualization? Elizabeth O'Connor says, "When we talk about being true to ourselves—being the persons we are intended to be—we are talking about gifts."[3] I begin to consider the area of gifts in search of an answer. Out of the excess of my reading and discussion certain thoughts repeatedly emerge.

> The determination of our gifts may involve struggle. Our inner peace will be the most reliable indication we are on the right track.
> Comparisons, envy and the fear of other's envy can throw us off the track. The answer is within ourselves. "We are not better for another man's praise nor worse for his blame."[4]
> The development of one gift may necessitate the sacrifice of another.
> Our gifts, if exercised, multiply.

How does all this fit together with the improbabilities of my life situation? Being the person I am "intended to be" necessitates an evaluation of my responsibilities. How can there be a sense of rightness if I exercise my gifts at the expense of my responsibilities? Responsibilities must take top priority. It would be ideal if I could exercise my gifts in the fulfilling of these responsibilities. But it is not always possible.

Yet, if God puts in man the creative seeds, wouldn't it follow that He would not intend for them to be neglected? Our hearts, as well as our minds must be nurtured; our souls as well as our bodies must be clothed. We should try to nurture our gifts in whatever time we can find. But there may be stretches of time in our lives when that is not possible. Will our souls die of starvation? How could it be that in doing what is right, we die in spirit?

Could it be that investing our very tasks with creative energy and approaching our relationships with beauty and dignity might in and of itself be an exercising of gifts? And isn't it possible, as different situations demand different skills, the fulfilling of my responsibilities may call forth gifts I would never otherwise have realized? (I have not closed off the possibility that a woman could pursue a career and fulfill her responsibilities to home and family.

But not without certain sacrifices. Sacrifices I am not willing to make at this point.)

Does it then follow that the development of gifts unrelated to the call of duty must be sacrificed? Do I simply table them as incongruous to this stage of my life—something to be resumed when the children are all in school or even out of the home? Or after (and if) I have first cared for all others?

I find I'm no more willing to abandon the development of specific gifts now that my priority is home, than I was willing to give up home interests in my pre-children days when teaching was my primary concern. But I would deceive myself if I claim I can pursue these interests with the same single-mindedness and with the same results. Somewhere between the extremes of the feminist bent on her own fulfillment at any cost, and the homemaker committed to duty, there must be a place for me.

I think it comes down to an attitude. Because at this point in my life my priority is creating a home for my family, it would naturally follow that those other areas will be secondary. They are subject to interruptions, which will affect the quantity of my achievements in contrast to the professional. But I don't believe the quality must be sacrificed. Yet it is imperative that they be pursued for intrinsic satisfaction, not for tangible results.

Anne Morrow Lindbergh brings valuable insight to this problem in her book *The Flower and the Nettle*. In a letter written in 1937 she suggests that "when a woman succeeds in combining a career with home-life, it is at the price of a pigeonholed life—a man's life. Because in order to compete with men they must concentrate their energies into a narrow line. And I think in doing that they deny themselves the special attributes and qualities of women." She goes on to develop woman as a circle—"rounded and receptive and sensitive in all directions. I think they should be perceptive and aware and open to many currents and calls and—yes, even distractions. I think they must be content, or wise enough, to work for something much bigger and much more tangible, something that includes husbands and children and homes and background and character—and work too. But the work is only part of it, only a spoke in the wheel without which, perhaps,

193

the wheel won't go round as well, but not an end in itself, not a straight-line objective."[5]

I do have limits. But limits of my own choosing, not restrictions to which I must acquiesce. That makes all the difference. Even as I am beginning to see some open spaces with the children becoming more self-sufficient, it is unlikely as a married woman I will choose the "straight-line approach" of the professional except for limited periods of time. Yet it is possible that from the circle could emerge something unique, something special—not in spite of that approach, but because of it.

THE BALANCED LIFE

My writing possesses me. I go to church and think about my subject. Come home and make lunch. Children nap. I write. They awaken. I write. Vaguely I get raisins for Jonathan, coffee for Dave and me. I kiss a hurt ankle for Kimberly.

But all the time I'm writing. Ideas keep turning over in my mind. I'm in bondage. Why have I put this upon myself? Why even let myself deal with ideas that create tension within me? Tension that words alone can resolve.

> This above all—ask yourself in the stillest hour of your night; must I write? Delve into yourself for a deep answer. And if this should be affirmative, if you may meet this earnest question with a strong and simple "I must," then build your life according to this necessity; your life even into its most indifferent and slightest hour must be a sign of this urge and a testimony to it.[6]

That was written to a young poet—not to a mother of young children! Writing is out of proportion to the rest of life. I go through all the appropriate motions, but inwardly the thoughts spin and turn. It's as if all along the ideas have been formulating, building to a point where they must be expressed. Once I am committed to setting the thoughts on paper, they spill out and must be caught. On paper they are safe. In time I can expand, organize, refine—but I must "catch" them now.

So easily the "room of my own" spoke of the wheel can take over. I must impose balance on my life by setting up disciplines that will moderate my time. I must determine writing to be out of bounds if it *habitually* encroaches on routines required for a

195

smooth-running household, interferes with the people in my life, throws off activities I consider essential to a balanced life.

On the other hand I must enforce routines that protect the "room of my own" spoke.

Balance. It seems to come down to the balanced life. Like a tightrope artist I must walk the line stretched out before me, placing one foot carefully before the other. When I find myself leaning too far to one side, I must shift my weight so once again I can regain my delicate, my precarious balance. Never static. Balance . . .

In union with Christ all things find their proper place.[7]

SISTERS OF THE HEART

A knock on the back door. The front doorbell rings. My Tuesday morning circle friends are coming, laden with goodies—homemade Hungarian coffee cake, cinnamon-orange crescent rolls, quiche Lorraine, bowls of fruit . . . An egg soufflé is slipped into a previously warmed oven. Perking coffee competes with the aroma of good food.

We gather in the living room to share favorite inspirational readings and thoughts. As they talk I slip off and fill the glasses with ice water, set out plates of food. I can hear their voices as I move from room to room. My heart is filled with love for these women—my sisters of the heart. ("Have we not all one father? Hath not one God created us?"[8]) We share such common ground. So seldom do we have an opportunity to meet together; and when we do, it is limited in time, filled with interruptions. Yet there is an unspoken recognition of our need for each other. We draw strength from our mutual experience. Soon we will return to our separate worlds, resume our individual responsibilities—these moments are all the more valued for their rarity.

What a joy it is to embrace friends in the lovely order of our home. They know better—they've been here before! They're eye-witnesses of toy-strewn rooms, kitchen cluttered with dirty dishes, unswept floors. All the confusion of everyday living. No, they are not deceived by such order. And that is not my intent. I would hope to create, if only for one morning, an atmosphere of calm and beauty. And I would pray that from this time together we would each receive an inner calm and order to carry back to our busy lives.

Women friends—sisters of the heart!

SOLITUDE

I am depleted. Giving bits and pieces of myself to this and that, I suddenly realize there is nothing left to give. Emptied of inner resources, I keep going through the motions. I know my "offerings" have ceased to be unique. Homemaking is a duty performed. My dealings with the children are determined by expedience alone. Creativity no longer exists for me. The well has run dry!

Yet I cannot stop. Not now. Responsibilities that cannot be postponed have converged at one time. Doctor's appointments to make and keep. Costumes to prepare. Weeds to pull. Letters to write. The washing piles up. Mending. Seasonal clothing must be sorted out. Extra meetings to attend. The phone keeps on ringing. Routines must be maintained. My spirit gives out before my body. So I keep going, going, going . . .

I know what has gone wrong. I have continued to give out without renewing my inner resources. Can one breathe out without breathing in? I need to draw apart from everyone, everything, and nourish my soul. I've told myself solitude is a luxury I can't afford. But my poverty of spirit declares solitude as necessary for my soul as food is for the body. Solitude. A time to remove myself from distraction. To order my day. My week. My life. To get in touch with myself. With my Maker.

I think of Anne Morrow Lindbergh's reflections triggered by the moon shell.

> You will say to me solitude. You will remind me that I must try to be alone for part of each year, even a week or a few days; and for part of each day, even for an hour or a few minutes in order to keep my core, my center, my island-quality. You will remind me that unless I keep the island-quality in-

tact somewhere within me, I will have little to give my husband, my children, my friends or the world at large.[9]

I must carve out of my day, time, and label it solitude. It has not been allotted to me by virtue of my calling. No one can give it to me. I must take it and guard it as one would a rare treasure.

NOT ENOUGH TIME

> I still find each day too short for all the thoughts I want to think, all the walks I want to take, all the books I want to read, and all the friends I want to see.[10]

The words leap out at me from the competing messages of the one thousand cards neatly lined up on display racks. I reach for the card. My mind races with thoughts sympathetic to this message.

"Each day is too short for all the thoughts I want to think . . ." Not grand Original Thoughts. Just putting together the loose ends of my thinking. Sorting out information I have been bombarded with from the news media, my reading, and conversations. Input on current issues—the Middle East crisis, economics, energy, the Equal Rights Amendment. I have picked up bits and pieces, here and there. "Someday I'll work this through. Come up with some sort of synthesis. Have a point of view." Instead, thoughts float without a center, subject to the most recent input. I must think about this, I say to myself. Instead I talk, imposing on other persons half-developed opinions, poorly substantiated.

"Each day is too short for all the walks I want to take . . ." Alone. With the family. Hike the nature path around the lake. Feed the ducks. Leisurely walks from here to nowhere—to say nothing of the rides! Search out faraway spots to antique—dig up hidden treasures. Excursions to area attractions. Concerts. Plays. Ideas aplenty from me. Oh yes. I make the plans. Dream the dreams. But when can I *do* them?

"Each day is too short for all the books I want to read . . ." Favorite books. Friends of a sort—sitting on bookshelves, waiting to be revisited. The growing stack of books I purchased with the promise of relaxed reading. Required reading—for a book club, a study group. Musts. And then there is that nameless category of books compiled from references made in other readings. The recommended. Current best reading. I hold firmly to my dream of long, uninterrupted evenings—reading, reading, reading.

Friends—we touch briefly in passing. "We'll have to get together soon. It's been so long." When we do meet, our time is punctuated by interruptions from children, orchestrated by The Schedule. Only an echo of years past—talks late into the night unencumbered by Responsibilities. I think of friends far away—the volumes I intend to write to them. Instead they receive our annual Christmas card with my promise "I'll write more later—after Christmas." (I can imagine them closing the card and saying knowingly, "Maybe.") Then there are the acquaintances. Those people with whom each contact brings a good connection. The feeling we could be friends. Yes, yes, "each day *is* too short for all the friends I want to see."

Not enough hours in the day, the week, the year for all the things I want to do. So I eke out a moment when I can, or steal a moment when I can't, to fit in one of these luxuries. For luxuries they are indeed.

I tell myself it is good this way—maybe better this way. Would I have the good judgment to balance these luxuries if they were not moderated by the necessities of life? Or would I like a greedy child stuff myself to my fill, till satiated with pleasure I could no longer taste at all? (Try me, I counter.)

No. Even now I can see because of their scarcity, these things are all the more precious. Like the sweet brief moments of a rose in full bloom, all the more cherished for the brevity of its life span.

And is it not the promise of such moments that sends me flying through my work? That checks me from the aimless frittering away of hours? "When I have finished this chore I will read the next chapter." Or write a letter, go for that walk. Memories of past pleasures sustain me through the routines; anticipation spurs me on.

No, not even a lifetime contains enough hours for all those things I'd like to do. And I'm glad. For the moment I cease to anticipate is the moment I'll have ceased to really live. I will treasure my dreams and plans not just for the hope of fulfillment, but for what they represent to me of the rich, boundless opportunities of living!

THE ORDERED LIFE

"And let our ordered lives confess the beauty of Thy peace."[11] The ordered life—reasoned, disciplined, temperate. So often this ideal is at variance with the realities of my life—a life marked by fragmentation, clutter, and distraction.

It is order I need. Order strong enough to govern my circumstances, vigorous enough to integrate the divergent parts of my life. Not a radical burst of self-discipline, austere and rigid, but order, flexible and tempered by love.

Is it possible for me to lead anything close to an ordered life with any degree of consistency? Or is that one more aspiration that can only be realized later, when my life is less complicated? If that time ever comes.

I believe it is possible now, but only as a by-product of a deeper inner order. An order that comes from having things at peace within myself—a kind of equilibrium where the inner and outward man are at one.

If the things of the spirit are not first put in order, it seems that no effort on my part is sufficient to consistently regulate the details of daily living. It is essential that I daily turn to the "Father of men's souls" to restore order to my mind and spirit. As He reorders me from within, outwardly things begin to take shape. The spirit of the day is not conducive to this kind of attention to the inner man, but from experience I know it to be a necessity.

> Dear Lord and Father of mankind,
>   Forgive our foolish ways;
> Reclothe us in our rightful mind,
> In purer lives Thy service find,
>   In deeper reverence, praise.

Drop Thy still dews of quietness
  Till all our strivings cease;
Take from our souls the strain and stress,
And let our ordered lives confess
  The beauty of Thy peace.[12]

Open Letter to My Daughter

Dear Kimberly,

Sweet sleeping child. So small, so vulnerable. This day has brought to me an aching sense of the passing of time. Just one more day of living, but with one great difference—you are a year older. Today we celebrated your fifth birthday. Remnants of the festivities are scattered throughout the house. Streamers, balloons, torn gift wrappings. It has been a big day. It is one exhausted five-year-old slumbering here before me.

Kimberly, you know by now life is not all pink balloons and streamers. But all in all, life has been pretty good to you. I wish I could promise you it will always go on this way. I can't. How I wish I could go ahead of you to guide, warn, and protect you. "Walk out" the hard parts for you. I can't. And even if I could, it wouldn't be right. No, I must free you to live life yourself—whatever that may involve.

Yet there are lessons I want to teach you to equip you for living. Lessons that are being woven through most of our dealings with you. Can you hear them? Or will you, like me, have to learn these lessons for yourself from the school of life? I will state them, my dear, not only that you may someday read them and understand, but as a present reminder to me of what things really are important.

I would hope to communicate to you a deeper understanding of happiness than things going your way. All through life, things will be held before you with the promise of giving happiness. But the happiness I desire for you is the "pure, deep-flowing joy that springs out of maturity and fulfillment."[1] Happiness cannot be purchased cheaply. It is the by-product of living life to your fullest potential within the boundaries of rightness.

May you learn the underlying principle of acceptance. Not a passive acquiescence to whatever may be. But a recognition that no situation, place, or person is perfect. When you have determined your "given," make the most of it, whether it is for a day or for a lifetime. You will lose valuable living time waiting for what, in fact, may never be.

You can change. It's true, Kimberly. No matter what you hear about behavior and determinism, you can change. I know, I have. And I am still changing. My respect for the human will continues to increase.

Biblical principles work. They are the Creator's set of directions for His creation. We malfunction when we don't follow the Instructor's Manual. I can add no more to that.

May you recognize the high value of right relationships. It is significant that the two greatest commandments Christ issued were relational in nature. "Love thy neighbor as thyself" is second only to "Love the Lord thy God with all thy heart, soul, and mind." Love—it will require you to give up your rights at times for something bigger—right relationships. God, knowing our fickleness, has given us laws of love to carry us when the feelings of love falter.

I would be remiss if I did not speak to you of being a woman. There are those who sentimentalize the woman. Endow her with soft, endearing qualities. Ideals. Others speak bitterly of injustices served her, seek to liberate her. I reject both extremes. Not because either is untrue, but because to concentrate at this level makes the issue too small.

I can't deny that women have suffered a kind of discrimination. Yes, there are disadvantages to being a woman. But that is the way it is with everything—to be one is not to be another. And all that goes with it. *That* is the underlying issue.

I have found the positive aspects of being a woman to overwhelmingly offset the disadvantages. But you must discover for yourself what it means for you to be a woman. Come face to face with your feminine distinctiveness and get that squared away in a manner you can live with.

Then you will be free to acknowledge our common humanity—male and female; how in our human qualities we are so very much the same. Emphasize and be tender toward your complement—man. To women—likewise. Do not compete, but contribute out of your uniqueness to all humankind.

These are big lessons, dear. Lessons that take a lifetime of learning. I will try to facilitate your learning by being the person and the parent God wants me to be. As a person I will try to demonstrate these truths at the action level. As a parent I will try to guide you effectively by setting limits and consistently enforcing them; saying yes whenever I can, and saying no no more than is necessary; helping you avoid the choices that have serious consequences, without overprotecting you from growth-producing mistakes; supporting you through difficult situations without unnecessarily smoothing the way or "going to bat" for you; helping you find out who you are, rather than imposing on you my dreams. Yes, Kimberly, I'll try . . .

But I know full well I can't be all things to you. It hurts me to say that. I know that no matter how hard I try there will be times I'll hurt you just by who I am. I pray you will forgive me where I have not been right for you, or where my own selfishness has interfered with your best interest. As you witness my limitations perhaps you can learn without too many scars that no one can meet the needs of another fully. Only God. That you will not expect of any relationship—friend, husband, child—more than you should. It can only hurt you—hurt them.

Instead, search deeply within yourself, and deal honesty with what you find. Don't be afraid of what you see, for until you see things as they are you cannot deal with them and become the person you are meant to be. Should you find sin, confess it. Love. Give it freely within the limits set by God for your own good. Should you see dreams and visions, seek God's direction in the realization of all that is good.

The day may come when you challenge our values. Perhaps even our faith. I hope I'll be equal to it, recognizing it to be as necessary a part of the process for you as it was for me. I will pray daily that God will lead you into His Truth, and into loving relationship with Him.

I can't hand you easy answers, guaranties, or escape from heart-aches. You may face problems that seem without rational solution. But I can promise you that God is sufficient for every conceivable situation. He can give you a peace and joy that transcend the most difficult circumstance.

As I look at you with my heart full of love, I realize now why my mother equipped me to face the world with one passage from Scripture. It was as much a comfort for her as an assurance for me. I can think of nothing better to pass on to you than the same set of directions for success my mother gave me on my college graduation day.

> This book of the law shall not depart out of thy mouth; but thou shalt meditate therein day and night, that thou mayest observe to do according to all that is written therein: for then thou shalt make thy way prosperous, and then thou shalt have good success.
>
> Have not I commanded thee? Be strong and of good courage, be not afraid, neither be thou dismayed: for the Lord thy God is with thee whithersoever thou goest.[2]

Kimberly, you have been five years of sheer joy to Daddy and me. Your resourcefulness and spunky independence never cease to delight us. A natural peacemaker, you so often make things right by your gentle, loving spirit. I may write the lessons, dear, but in so many ways you teach me of living, of loving.

Sleep on, little one. Tomorrow soon will be here. You will play with your presents, each in its turn; and you will glory in being five years old.

I love you,

Mother

Notes

Chapter 1

Home—"A Safe Place"

1. P. D. Eastman, *The Best Nest* (Random House, Inc., 1968), p. 3.
2. Blaise Pascal, *Pascal's Pensées* (E. P. Dutton & Co., Inc., 1958), paperback edition, No. 552, p. 150.
3. *Milambu Ya Bababa* (Communauté Presbytérienne au Zaire, Kananza, République du Zaire, 1959), pamphlet.
4. Robert Browning, "Pippa Passes," *The Treasury of Religious Verse* (Fleming H. Revell Company, 1962).
5. Marjorie Holmes, *I've Got to Talk to Somebody, God* (Doubleday & Company, Inc., 1968), pp. 36, 37.
6. Elisabeth Elliot, *Let Me Be a Woman* (Tyndale House Publishers, Inc., 1976), p. 64.
7. Proverbs 18:10, New American Standard Version.

Chapter 2

Memory Building

1. Edith Schaeffer, *What Is a Family?* (Fleming H. Revell Company, 1975), p. 197.
2. Richard Le Gallienne, "I Meant to Do My Work Today," *My Poetry Book, an Anthology of Modern Verse for Boys and Girls* (John C. Winston Co., 1934).
3. Elisabeth Elliot, *Let Me Be a Woman* (Tyndale House Publishers, Inc., 1976), pp. 116, 117.
4. Matthew 25:40, King James Version.
5. Christina Rossetti, "In the Bleak Midwinter."

6. Emily Dickinson, "There Is No Frigate Like a Book," *The Poems of Emily Dickinson*, edited by Bianchi and Hampson (Little, Brown, 1937).
7. Robert McCloskey, *Make Way for Ducklings* (The Viking Press, Inc., 1941).
8. Gladys Hunt, *Honey for a Child's Heart* (Zondervan Publishing House, 1969), pp. 14, 21.

Chapter 3

TRUE CREATIVITY

1. Paul Tournier, *A Place for You* (Harper & Row, Publishers, Inc., 1968), p. 107.
2. Romans 12:2, King James Version.
3. Psalm 138:13–16, New American Standard Version.
4. William J. Gaither, "You're Something Special," *The Bill Gaither Trio—Especially for Children* (Impact Records, 1973).
5. Paul Tournier, *The Adventure of Living* (Harper & Row, Publishers, Inc., 1965), p. 19.
6. Joan Walsh Anglund, *Morning Is a Little Child* (Harcourt, Brace & World, Inc., 1969).
7. Edith Schaeffer, *What Is a Family?* (Fleming H. Revell Company, 1975), p. 59.
8. Ibid., pp. 61, 62.
9. *A Dozen Little Plays* (Parents' Magazine Press, 1965).
10. Mary O'Neill, *Hailstones and Halibut Bones* (Doubleday & Company, Inc., 1961), pp. 43, 44.
11. James Dobson, *Hide or Seek* (Fleming H. Revell Company, 1974), p. 74.
12. Ibid., p. 73.
13. Carl Sandburg, "Fog," *Golden Treasury of Poetry*, selected by Louis Untermeyer (Western Publishing Co., Inc., 1959).
14. Romans 1:20, Today's English Version.

Chapter 4

THE SHAPING OF CHARACTER

1. Proverbs 22:15, King James Version.
2. Colossians 3:20, King James Version.

3. Bruce Narramore, *Help! I'm a Parent* (Zondervan Corporation, 1972). Chapter 8, "Choosing the Right Method of Discipline."
4. T. Berry Brazilton, Professor of Pediatrics, Harvard Medical School.
5. Paul Tournier, *The Adventure of Living* (Harper & Row, Publishers, Inc., 1965), paperback edition, p. 148.
6. James 1:5, Today's English Version.
7. Deuteronomy 6:5–9, King James Version.
8. Deuteronomy 6:6, 7a, King James Version.

Chapter 5

THE FAMILY—A GREENHOUSE FOR RELATIONSHIPS

1. Catherine Marshall, "How I'm Raising My Second Family," *Good Housekeeping,* January, 1968, p. 129.
2. Elisabeth Elliot, *Let Me Be a Woman* (Tyndale House Publishers, Inc., 1976), p. 95.
3. James Dobson, *Dare to Discipline* (Tyndale House Publishers, Inc., 1970), p. 21.
4. Edith Schaeffer, *What Is a Family?* (Fleming H. Revell Company, 1975), p. 74.
5. Psalm 101:2, Living Bible.
6. Elisabeth Elliot, *Let Me Be a Woman* (Tyndale House Publishers, Inc., 1976), p. 73.
7. William Shakespeare, *As You Like It,* (Act III, Scene V, Line 57).
8. Florida Scott-Maxwell, *Women and Sometimes Men* (Alfred A. Knopf, 1957).
9. Phyllis Theroux, "How to Find the Joy of Being Yourself," *House & Garden,* February 1978, p. 104.
10. Rainer Maria Rilke, *Letters to a Young Poet* (W. W. Norton & Company, Inc., 1934).

Chapter 6

"GROWTH OF A SOUL"

1. Catherine Marshall, *Beyond Ourselves* (McGraw-Hill Book Company, Inc., 1961, p. 70.
2. Jeremiah 29:13, New American Standard Version.

3. John R. Stott, *Basic Christianity* (The Inter-Varsity Fellowship, 1958), paperback edition, p. 18.
4. John Wesley's prayer room (Gordon Fraser postcard).
5. Scripture Union, *Encounter with God* Bible Study notes. Subscription address: 1716 Spruce St., Philadelphia, Pa. 19103.
6. Dag Hammarskjöld, *Markings* (Alfred A. Knopf, Inc., and Faber and Faber, Ltd. 1964), p. 122.
7. II Timothy 1:7, King James Version.
8. Philippians 4:6a, 7, New American Standard Version.
9. Elisabeth Elliot, "The Glory of God's Will," Wheaton College Chapel Talk, printed in the *Wheaton Alumni*, February 1977.
10. Romans 8:28, King James Version.
11. Corrie ten Boom, with John and Elizabeth Sherrill, *The Hiding Place* (Chosen Books, 1971), paperback edition, p. 178.
12. Paul Tournier, *The Adventure of Living* (Harper & Row, Publishers, Inc., 1965), paperback edition, p. 116.
13. Ibid., p. 195.
14. Paul Tournier, *The Healing of Persons* (Harper & Row, Publishers, Inc., 1965), p. 161.
15. Matthew 6:12.
16. James 1:2, 3, Phillips Modern English.
17. Philippians 4:8, New English Bible.
18. James 1:4, 5, Phillips Modern English.
19. Karen Maines, *Open Heart, Open Home* (David C. Cook Publishing Co., 1976), p. 69.
20. Andrae Crouch, "Through It All" (Manna Music, Inc., 1971).
21. Paul Tournier, *The Healing of Persons* (Harper & Row, Publishers, Inc., 1965), p. 236.
22. Acts 3:19, Phillips Modern English.
23. John Bailey, *A Diary of Private Prayer* (Charles Scribner's Sons, 1949), p. 15.
24. Psalm 51:10–12, King James Version.
25. Paul Tournier, *The Adventure of Living* (Harper & Row, Publishers, Inc., 1965), paperback edition, pp. 149, 150.
26. Exodus 33:13a, 14, King James Version.
27. Catherine Marshall, *Beyond Ourselves* (McGraw-Hill Book Company, Inc., 1961), p. 128.
28. Elisabeth Elliot, *A Slow and Certain Light* (Word Books, 1973), p. 25.
29. Joshua 1:8, King James Version.
30. Thomas à Kempis, *Imitation of Christ* (Grosset & Dunlap), revised edition, p. 270.
31. Colossians 2:6, Today's English Version.
32. Hebrews 12:10, Phillips Modern English (early edition, 1960).

Chapter 7

A ROOM OF MY OWN

1. Gladys Hunt, *MS Means Myself* (Zondervan Publishing House, 1972), pp. 46, 47.
2. A. A. Milne, "Disobedience," *When We Were Very Young*, (E. P. Dutton & Co., Inc., 1924), paperback edition, p. 33.
3. Elizabeth O'Connor, *The Eighth Day of Creation* (Word Books, 1971), p. 14.
4. William Blake as quoted by Elizabeth O'Connor, ibid., p. 49.
5. Ann Morrow Lindbergh, *The Flower and the Nettle* (Harcourt, Brace, Jovanovich, Inc., 1976), pp. 124, 125.
6. Rainer Maria Rilke, *Letters to a Young Poet* (W. W. Norton & Company, Inc., 1934), pp. 18, 19.
7. Colossians 1:17, Today's English Version.
8. Malachi 2:10a, King James Version.
9. Anne Morrow Lindbergh, *Gift from the Sea* (Pantheon Books, 1955), pp. 58, 59.
10. John Burroughs.
11. John Greenleaf Whittier, "Dear Lord and Father of Mankind," *The Hymnbook*: Presbyterian Church in the U.S. (Houghton Mifflin Company, authorized publisher), p. 416.
12. Ibid.

Final Notes

OPEN LETTER TO MY DAUGHTER

1. Catherine Marshall, *Beyond Ourselves* (McGraw-Hill Book Company, Inc., 1961), p. 10.
2. Joshua 1:8, 9, King James Version.

216